CW00540741

David L Jones

First published in 2023 by Reed New Holland Publishers
Sydney

Level 1, 178 Fox Valley Road, Wahroonga, NSW 2076, Australia

newhollandpublishers.com

A record of this book is held at the National Library of Australia.

ISBN 978 1 92554 688 0

Managing Director: Fiona Schultz
Publisher and Project Editor: Simon Papps
Designer: Andrew Davies
Production Director: Arlene Gippert

Printed in China

10 9 8 7 6 5 4 3 2 1

Keep up with Reed New Holland and New Holland Publishers on Facebook

 ReedNewHolland
 @ReedNewHolland

Front cover: Lemon-scented Bloodwood, *Corymbia citriodora*.

Page 1: Desert Ghost Gum, *Corymbia aparrerinja*.

Page 3: Leopardwood or Bagala, *Flindersia maculosa*.

Back cover: Moodjar, *Nuytsia floribunda*.

TREES
of Australia

CONTENTS

INTRODUCTION

The number of different species of tree that are native to
Australia is estimated to be in the thousands and so the coverage
in such a tiny book as this must be very limited. This book
includes 180 species of Australian native trees and includes
diverse groups such as eucalypts, wattles, casuarinas, conifers,
melaleucas, palms, pandans, grass trees and even a fern. With
so many species of trees in Australia, and trees occurring in
such a diverse range of habitats, the selection is biased towards
trees that I have encountered during my botanical travels. Iconic
Australian trees such as Red Cedar and River Red Gum are
included as well as many common species, popular cultivated
trees, elusive trees of the rainforest and a few that deserve to
become better known. The photos are all mine except for my
daughter Sandie's shots of *Nuytsia*.

Tree height: For convenience the height of trees as considered in
this book are: **Small**, 6–10m; **Medium**, 10–30m; **Tall**, 30–50m;
and **Very tall**, over 50m.

Tree names: The text includes at least one common name
of each tree as well as a designated binomial name, which
consists of a **genus** name and **species** epithet. For example the
common name Silky Oak is associated with the botanical name
of *Grevillea robusta*, *Grevillea* being the name of the genus and
robusta being the species name. Botanically, binomial names
are more accurately applied than common names, which often
arise from general useage or popularity. A tree can have several

common names but only a single accurate binomial name. The common names used in this book are those that are widely adopted or commonly accepted.

Arrangement of the trees: The trees included in this book are arranged by their botanical names within their plant family and the plant families are arranged alphabetically throughout the text.

AKA	also known as.	Qld	Queensland
c.	circa, approximately	Ra.	ranges
Dec, Jan	December, January, etc	S(s)	south
		SA	South Australia
E(e)	east	sp.	species singular
Is.	island(s)	spp.	species plural
N(n)	north	Tas	Tasmania
NCal	New Caledonia	tlnds.	tablelands
NG	New Guinea	Vic	Victoria
NSW	New South Wales	W(w)	west
NT	Northern Territory	WA	Western Australia

IMPORTANT GROUPS OF AUSTRALIAN NATIVE TREES

Two groups deserve special mention: the genus *Acacia* and the Eucalypts.

Acacia (family Mimosaceae)

A large and complex group of heterogeneous shrubs and trees that dominate the Australian flora. Wattles have spread all over Australia from coastal dunes to inland deserts and subalpine forests, but they are most prominent in drier semi-arid areas, even replacing *Eucalyptus* as the dominant group in some habitats. Growth habits vary tremendously in such a large and diverse group of plants, from prostrate shrubs to tall trees. True wattle leaves are bipinnate and can be seen in most species at the seedling stage. One distinctive group of wattles retains its bipinnate leaves to maturity but for the vast majority of species the seedling bipinnate leaves are rapidly replaced by modified petioles (phyllodes) which form leaf-like structures capable of transpiration and photosynthesis. A small group of wattles have neither bipinnate leaves nor phyllodes, the role being taken over by modified stems (cladodes) which act like leaves. Wattle flowers are mostly in shades of cream or yellow and, although tiny, are grouped in globular heads or cylindrical spikes that often provide a conspicuous display. The seeds, some of which include an edible aril, are carried in pods (legumes) which spilt when ripe. According to recent studies, there are about 1,350 species of *Acacia* in the world, and about 1,000 of these occur in Australia.

Zig-zag Wattle, *Acacia macradenia*.

The Eucalypts (family Myrtaceae)

In this book I use the word eucalypt as a general term covering the Myrtaceous genera *Angophora*, *Corymbia* and *Eucalyptus*. These shrubs and trees dominate the Australian forests. *Angophora* and *Corymbia* have been included within the genus *Eucalyptus* at times, but both genera have also been segregated based on distinctive botanical features.

Angophora: Both the juvenile and adult leaves are arranged in opposite pairs; the flowers have tiny sepals reduced to vestigial bumps, and overlapping petals; significantly the sepals and petals are not fused to form the cap-like operculum so prominent in the buds of *Eucalyptus*; the fruit are thin papery capsules that are often ribbed. There are nine species of *Angophora*, all in eastern Australia.

Corymbia: The juvenile leaves and those formed on regrowth shoots are opposite and differ from the adult leaves which are arranged alternately along the branchlets; the five sepals are fused on form an inner operculum in the bud and the five petals are fused to form an outer cap (operculum), thus the flowers have no obvious petals but the numerous white or colourful stamens are fully exposed when the operculum is shed; the inflorescence branches in such a way that the buds and flowers (often in groups of seven) end up at more or less the same level (flat-topped). There are about 100 species of *Corymbia* distributed widely in Australia, including the tropics. Bloodwoods, ghost gums and spotted gums are important groups.

Eucalyptus: The juvenile leaves and those formed on regrowth shoots are usually in opposite pairs and differ from the adult leaves which are usually arranged so as to appear alternately along the branchlets; however, some species of *Eucalyptus* have opposite leaves at maturity and some species of *Eucalyptus* retain the juvenile leaves for life; buds are covered by a cap (operculum) formed either by the fusion of the sepals or petals, or both; this cap covers the numerous white or colourful stamens and is forced off when the stamens expand prior to the flower opening; the woody capsules (gumnuts) have apical valves that open to release the seeds. There are about 800 species of *Eucalyptus*, the vast majority native to Australia.

DECIDUOUS NATIVE TREES

The term deciduous, when applied to plants, refers to the falling off or shedding of parts caused by seasonal changes. In the case of trees, it is commonly applied to broad-leaved species which shed their leaves in autumn to avoid the excesses of cold winters. Deciduous trees of this type are found in several areas of the world, especially in the Northern Hemisphere and high-altitude habitats in Asia, but this growth feature is not generally associated with the Australian flora. Deciduous plants, however, do occur in Australia. *Nothofagus gunnii* from Tasmania is renowned for its autumnal leaf colours prior to leaf shedding in winter. It is often promoted as Australia's only deciduous plant, but many other native species shed their leaves so as to avoid seasonal excesses. In Red Cedar, which is famed for the quality of its timber, the leaves, which turn yellow before shedding, provided vital locality clues to the timber getters of the last century chasing its prized wood. Many more deciduous trees and shrubs occur in the Australian tropics where monsoonal climates prevail. In these climates the vast majority of the rainfall occurs during the relatively short summer (termed the wet season), which is followed by a long dry winter period (termed the dry season). Many plants in these tropical dry forests and monsoon forests shed their leaves partially or fully as a survival mechanism during the dry winter period to reduce water loss, and then renew growth after the first rains of the wet season. Several species also flower while leafless or soon after new growth occurs.

Tanglefoot, *Nothofagus gunnii*.

Examples of deciduous native trees follow, ordered by family and then species:

Combretaceae: Beach Almond (*Terminalia catappa*), Mueller's Damson (*T. muelleri*), Yellow Wood (*T. oblongata*), Wild Plum (*T. platyphylla*), Damson Plum (*T. sericocarpa*).

Euphorbiaceae: Scrub Ironbark (*Bridelia leichhardtii*), Hairy Ironbark (*B. tomentosa*), Hard Cascarilla (*Croton arnhemica*), Tracey's Puzzle (*Margaritaria dubium-traceyi*).

Fabaceae: Leichhardt Bean (*Cassia brewsteri*), Bat's Wing Coral Tree (*Erythrina vespertilio*), Coastal Coral Tree (*E. insularis*), Bauhinia (*Lysiphyllum cunninghamii*), Malabar Bauhinia (*Piliostigma malabaricum*).

Lecythidaceae: Mango Pine (*Barringtonia calyptrata*), Cocky Apple (*Planchonia careya*).

Malvaceae: Australian Baobab (*Adansonia gregorii*), Cotton Tree (*Bombax ceiba*), Illawarra Flame Tree (*Brachychiton acerifolius*), Broad-leaved Bottle Tree (*B. australis*), Lacebark Tree (*B. discolor*), Queensland Bottle Tree (*B. rupestris*), Kapok Trees (*Cochlospermum fraseri* and *C. gillivraei*). Several other species of *Brachychiton* are deciduous or semi-deciduous: *B. albidus*, *B. chillagoensis*, *B. compactus*, *B. garrawayae*, *B. grandifolius*, *B. paradoxus* and *B. velutinosus*.

Meliaceae: White Cedar (*Melia azedarach*), Red Cedar (*Toona ciliata*).

Mimosaceae: Red Bead Tree (*Adenanthera pavonina*), Powderpuff Tree (*Albizia lebbeck*), Cape Laceflower (*Archidendron hirsutum*), Salmon Bean (*A. vaillantii*), Carthormion (*Carthormion umbellatum*), Red Siris (*Paraserianthes toona*).

Moraceae: Sandpaper Fig (*Ficus fraseri*), Rocky River Fig (*F. nodosa*), Cluster Fig (*F. racemosa*), Superb Fig (*F. henneana* var. *superba*), White Fig (*F. virens*).

Myrtaceae: Round-leaved Bloodwood (*Corymbia latifolia*), White Gum (*Eucalyptus platyphylla*).

Rubiaceae: Leichhardt Tree (*Nauclea orientalis*).

Simaroubaceae: White Siris (*Ailanthus triphysa*).

180 species accounts, arranged from A to Z by family, from Anarcardiaceae to Xanthorrhoeaceae

THE TREES

PINK POPLAR *Euroschinus falcatus*

Handsome fast-growing tree useful for shelter and shade in the tropics. Fruit eaten by birds.

SIZE/ID: 10–25 x 10–15m. Leaves pinnate, to 30cm long. Leaflets to 15 x 8cm, dark green, shiny. Flowers Sep–Nov, 5–6mm diam., white or pink, panicles. Drupes to 9mm across, black when ripe.

RANGE/HABITAT: Qld, NSW (Cooktown to Jervis Bay). Coast to ranges in open forest and drier rainforest.

16 BURDEKIN PLUM *Pleiogynium timorense*

Hardy dioecious tree with spreading shady canopy. Soft fruit
edible or made into jam.

SIZE/ID: 10–20 x 8–12m. Leaves pinnate,
to 28cm long. Leaflets to 10 x 6cm, dark
green, veins pale. Flowers Jan–Mar, 5mm
diam., yellow/green, short racemes. Drupes
to 3 x 4cm, red/purple/black (rarely white).

RANGE/HABITAT: Qld (Cape York to Gympie);
also NG, Pacific Is. Coast to ranges in scrub
and drier rainforest.

CANARY BEECH *Huberantha nitidissima*

Slow-growing tree with decorative shiny foliage, unusual flowers and colourful fruit. AKA *Polyalthia nitidissima*.

SIZE/ID: 10–18 x 4–8m. Bark grey/brown, flaky. Leaves to 14 x 6cm, dark green. Flowers Oct–Mar, 2–3cm diam., green/yellowish, fragrant, single or clusters. Berries to 14 x 9mm, orange/red.

RANGE/HABITAT: NT, Qld (Cape York to Clarence R.), NSW; also NG, NCal. Coast to ranges in drier rainforest and streambanks

18 MILKY PINE *Alstonia scholaris*

Fast-growing tree planted in parks and streets. Survives cyclones by shedding branches. Has medicinal properties.

SIZE/ID: 15–30 x 15–20m. Sap milky, sticky. Leaves to 22 x 7.5cm, in whorls, whitish beneath. Flowers Sep–Jan, 1cm diam., white/cream, fragrant, large clusters. Follicles to 45cm x 5mm, string-like, splitting to release plumed seeds.

RANGE/HABITAT: Tropical Qld, NT; also NG, Asia including China. Coast to ranges in rainforest.

RUBBER TREE *Cerbera manghas*

Bushy tree widely grown in coastal areas of the tropics. Leaves, fruit and seeds are very poisonous.

SIZE/ID: 6–12 x 5–8m. Sap milky, sticky. Leaves to 25 x 7cm. Flowers sporadic, 2.5–3.5cm diam., sweetly scented like frangipani, panicles. Drupes to 8 x 5cm, pink/red.

RANGE/HABITAT: Qld (Torres Strait Is to Noosa); also NG, Asia, Africa. Coastal scrub and rainforest.

20 **UMBRELLA TREE** *Heptopleurum actinophyllum*

Distinctive tree recognisable by its drooping glossy leaves and octopus-like flower heads. Birds and mammals feed on the flowers and fruit.

SIZE/ID: 10–20 x 8–12m. Leaves palmate; leaflets radiating, to 30 x 10cm. Inflorescence of clustered terminal racemes. Flowers Aug–Mar, 6mm diam., pink/red, in clusters. Drupes red, ribbed.

RANGE/HABITAT: Tropical Qld, NT; also NG. Coast to ranges and tlnds in wetter forests.

IVORY BASSWOOD *Polyscias australiana*

Distinctive slender tree with long leaves and large spreading/
drooping clusters of small flowers and fruit. Fruit eaten by birds.

SIZE/ID: 5–15 x 5–10m. Leaves pinnate, to 1.2m long. Leaflets
to 22 x 10cm. Flowers
Jul–May, 5–6mm diam.,
white/cream. Drupes
to 10mm diam., purple/
black.

RANGE/HABITAT: NT, Qld
(Cape York to Eumundi);
also NG. Coast to ranges
and tlnds in wetter
forests.

PENCIL CEDAR *Polyscias murrayi*

Decorative tree with cylindrical trunk, multi-branched umbrella-like crown and long fern-like leaves. Fruit eaten by birds and possums.

SIZE/ID: 15–25 x 10–15m. Leaves pinnate, to 2m long. Leaflets to 16 x 8cm. Flowers Mar–May, 2–3mm diam., white/cream, large panicles. Drupes 5–6mm diam., purple/blue/black.

RANGE/HABITAT: Qld, NSW, Vic (Cape York to Howe Range). Coast to ranges and tlnds in disturbed forest and rainforest.

BULL KAURI *Agathis microstachya*

Imposing conifer with straight, columnar trunk, scaly bark and cream/brown timber that polishes well. Restricted distribution. Valuable timber tree.

SIZE/ID: 20–40 x 10–20m. Leaves to 9 x 2.5cm, stiff, leathery. Male cones to 3cm long. Female cones to 12 x 10cm, round/ovoid, green.

RANGE/HABITAT:
Qld (Atherton TInd).
Rainforest.

QUEENSLAND KAURI *Agathis robusta*

Magnificent conifer planted in parks and larger gardens as a specimen tree. Important timber tree with decorative bark.

SIZE/ID: 20–40 x 10–25m. Leaves to 13 x 4cm, stiff, leathery. Male cones to 10cm long. Female cones to 15 x 10cm, ovoid, green.

RANGE/HABITAT: Qld (Atherton Tlnd and Fraser Is./Maryborough); also NG. Coast to ranges and tlnds in drier rainforest.

BUNYA PINE *Araucaria bidwillii*

Impressive stately conifer. Mature cones, which weigh up to 10kg, are a health hazard but contain hard-shelled nuts with a tasty kernel.

SIZE/ID: 30–45 x 20–30m. Leaves to 5 x 1cm, shiny, stiff, sharply tipped. Male cones 15–20cm long. Female cones to 30 x 20cm, ovoid, dark green.

RANGE/HABITAT: Qld (Mt Lewis and Bunya Mtns). Ranges and tlnds in rainforest.

HOOP PINE *Araucaria cunninghamii*

Long-lived conifer recognisable by horizontal hoops on its bark, symmetrical shape and whorled branches. Valuable timber for veneers and plywood.

SIZE/ID: 30–60 x 20–30m. Leaves to 20 x 3mm, dark green. Male cones to 8cm long, in clusters. Female cones to 10 x 7cm, green or brown.

RANGE/HABITAT: Qld, NSW (McIlwraith Ra. to Nambucca R.). Coast to ranges in scrub and rainforest.

CARPENTARIA PALM *Carpentaria acuminata*

Fast-growing elegant palm widely planted in the tropics. Flowers and fruits all year. Colourful fruit eaten by Torresian Imperial-Pigeons and fruit-bats.

SIZE/ID: 15–30m tall. Trunk to 20cm diam., grey. Fronds pinnate, to 4m long. Leaflets to 60cm long, narrow. Flowers small, cream, panicles to 1.5m long. Drupes 1.5cm diam., bright red.

RANGE/HABITAT: NT (n). Coastal rainforest and monsoon forests.

CAPE RIVER FAN PALM *Livistona lanuginosa*

Endangered palm known from small populations. Cultivated for its decorative form and large waxy leaves.

SIZE/ID: 10–20m tall. Trunk to 35cm diam., grey/brown. Fronds palmate, 3–4m long, pale blue/grey/green, woolly; blades to 2m wide, nearly circular, tips drooping. Flowers Mar–Nov, 1.5cm long, cream, large panicles. Drupes 3cm long, purple/black.

RANGE/HABITAT: Qld (Burdekin River area). Floodplains, soaks, pools and margins of ephemeral streams.

VICTORIA RIVER FAN PALM *Livistona victoriae*

Slender palm associated with spectacular red sandstone gorges and cliffs. Forms colonies in permanent seepage water.

SIZE/ID: 10–15m tall. Trunk to 30cm diam., grey. Fronds palmate, 2–3m long, pale blue/grey; blades to 1m wide, nearly circular. Flowers Mar–Dec, small, cream/yellow, panicles to 1.5m long. Drupes 1–1.5cm diam., dark red/brown.

RANGE/HABITAT: WA, NT (border region). Stream banks and sandstone gorges.

30 **FOXTAIL PALM** *Wodyetia bifurcata*

Decorative palm, highly restricted in nature but widely planted in the tropics.

SIZE/ID: 10–15m tall. Trunk to 25cm diam., grey. Crownshaft pale green. Fronds to 3m long; leaflets arranged on each side of main stem. Flowers c. 1cm long, cream, in panicles to 1.5m long. Drupes 60mm diam., bright red.

RANGE/HABITAT: Qld (Melville Range). Coastal granite hills in open forest and rainforest.

GOLDEN BOUQUET TREE *Deplanchea tetraphylla*

Showy flowering tree from the tropics. Nectar-rich flowers attract birds and flying-foxes. Wallabies eat fallen flowers.

SIZE/ID: 10–20 x 5–12m. Leaves large, to 35 x 18cm, hairy. Flowers 25–35mm long, bright yellow, crowded in showy terminal clusters. Capsules to 11 x 2.5cm, brown, with winged seeds.

RANGE/HABITAT: Qld (Torres Strait Is. to Townsville); also NG. Open forest and rainforest margins.

MANGO BARK *Canarium australianum*

Attractive dioecious tree with a spreading shady canopy. Ideal for coastal areas. Fruit eaten by birds.

SIZE/ID: 15–25 x 8–12m. Leaves pinnate, to 25cm long. Leaflets to 14 x 5cm. Flowers Nov–Jun, c.5mm diam., white/cream, fragrant, drooping racemes. Drupes 2–3cm long, blue/black, containing an edible seed.

RANGE/HABITAT: Tropical Qld, NT, WA; NG. Coast to ranges in dunes, open forest and rainforest.

COOKTOWN IRONWOOD
Erythrophleum chlorostachys

Useful shade and shelter tree in drier tropical areas. Leaves toxic to stock and can poison water sources. Decorative, termite-resistant wood.

SIZE/ID: 10–15 x 6–10m. Leaves bipinnate, to 30cm long. Leaflets to 8 x 8cm, nearly round. Flowers Sep–Nov, 4–6mm long, green/yellow, cylindrical spikes. Pods to 20 x 4cm, flat, brown/black.

RANGE/HABITAT: Tropical Qld, NT, WA. Woodland and rainforest margins.

WARRIOR BUSH *Apophyllum anomalum*

Tough small tree valued by pastoralists for stock fodder. Fruit eaten by birds and livestock. Host plant for Caper White butterflies.

SIZE/ID: 3–6 x 4–8m. Bark dark brown, furrowed. Young stems whitish with small leaves. Older branches leafless, spreading to drooping. Flowers Sep–Feb, 4–6mm diam., unisexual, cream/yellow, scented. Berries c. 5mm across, black.

RANGE/HABITAT: Qld, NSW. Semi-arid inland plains and woodland.

DESERT OAK *Allocasuarina decaisneana*

Iconic tree restricted to arid desert regions where its long roots can tap deep underground water. Young trees resemble drooping pillars.

SIZE/ID:
10–20 x 5–8m.
Dioecious. Bark
thick, corky,
fire-resistant.
Branchlets
segmented,
needle-like.
Leaves tiny, in
rings around
branchlets.
Flowers Mar–
Jun, unisexual,
red/brown,
fluffy.

RANGE/
HABITAT: NT
(se), SA (nw),
WA (central
w). Spinifex
grassland in
deep red sand.

36 **BULOKE** *Allocasuarina luehmannii*

Widespread sheoak with clean trunk, deeply fissured rough
bark and ascending branchlets. Often in pure stands. Distinctive
flattish cones on female trees. Very hard wood.

SIZE/ID:
10–20 x 5–10m.
Dioecious.
Branchlets
segmented,
needle-like.
Leaves tiny,
scale-like, in
rings around
branchlets.
Flowers Aug–
Oct, unisexual,
red/brown.

RANGE/HABITAT:
Qld, NSW,
Vic, SA. Inland
plains in sands
and clays.

FOREST OAK *Allocasuarina torulosa*

Attractive sheoak recognised by thick corky bark and drooping branchlets that turn reddish/brown or purplish in winter.

SIZE/ID: 10–18 x 4–8m. Dioecious. Branchlets segmented, needle-like. Leaves tiny, scale-like, in rings of 4 around branchlets. Flowers unisexual, females red, males brown. Cones warty.

RANGE/HABITAT: Qld, NSW (Iron Range to Jenolan Caves). Coastal hills to tlnds in wetter forests.

DROOPING SHEOAK *Allocasuarina verticillata*

Distinctive sheoak with rounded bushy crown and drooping branchlets. Occurs in many different habitats, including stunted trees on coastal headlands. Often grows in pure stands.

SIZE/ID: 5–10 x 5–10m. Dioecious. Branchlets segmented, needle-like. Leaves tiny, scale-like, in rings around branchlets. Flowers Jul–Sep, unisexual, brown.

RANGE/HABITAT: NSW, ACT, Vic, Tas, SA. Coast to ranges and inland slopes in grassy woodland.

RIVER OAK *Casuarina cunninghamiana* subsp. *cunninghamiana*

Imposing tree found along the banks of permanent freshwater streams from the tropics to temperate zones, often well inland from the coast. Planted in shelterbelts, parks and for riverine conservation.

SIZE/ID: 20–45 x 10–20m. Dioecious. Branchlets segmented, needle-like. Leaves tiny, scale-like, in rings around branchlets. Flowers Sep–Nov, unisexual, red/brown.

RANGE/HABITAT: Qld, NSW (Laura to Bega).

40 **COAST SHEOAK** *Casuarina equisetifolia* subsp. *equisetifolia*

Coastal sheoak with an upright habit, drooping branches and greyish foliage. Commonly planted for its ability to withstand hostile coastal conditions.

SIZE/ID:
10–30 x 10–20m. Dioecious. Branchlets segmented, needle-like. Leaves tiny, scale-like, in rings around branchlets. Flowers Sep–Nov, unisexual, red/brown.

RANGE/HABITAT:
Tropical NT, Qld (Darwin to Cairns); also Asia, Pacific. Exposed headlands, coastal dunes and beaches.

DAINTREE PINE *Gymnostoma australianum*

Although openly branched and candelabra-like with maturity, this fascinating small tree is mostly seen as a compact Christmas-tree-like plant with densely crowded bright green foliage. Small brown woody cones open to release winged seeds.

SIZE/ID: 5–7 x 3–5m. Dioecious. Branchlets needle-like. Leaves tiny, scale-like, in whorls of four. Flowers unisexual, pink/brown.

RANGE/HABITAT: Qld (Daintree R. to Cape Tribulation area). Open areas in tropical rainforest.

WEEPING IVORYWOOD *Siphonodon pendulus*

Interesting tree from the tropics with a narrow growth habit, strongly weeping branchlets and small inconspicuous flowers followed by relatively large fruit.

SIZE/ID: 8–15 x 4–8m. Leaves to 20 x 4.5cm, often curved, leathery. Flowers Jan–Mar, c.1cm diam., white, single or small groups. Drupes 4–5cm diam., globose, yellow/green.

RANGE/HABITAT: Qld (Cape York to Mareeba). Open forest and woodland, often near streams.

BEAUTY LEAF *Calophyllum inophyllum*

Stately tree common on tropical beaches and headlands where it tolerates strong salt-laden winds, even cyclones.

SIZE/ID: 12–25 x 10–15m. White/yellow sap. Leaves to 20 x 12cm, bright green, shiny.

Flowers 2–3cm diam., fragrant, white/cream petals, stamens orange/yellow. Drupes 3–5cm long, green to brown.

RANGE/HABITAT: Tropical Qld and NT; also NG and Pacific Is. Coastal scrub and littoral rainforest.

44 KAPOK TREE *Cochlospermum gillivraei*

Small, sparse tree with conspicuous clusters of yellow flowers when leafless. Seeds are attached to white kapok-like fibre.

SIZE/ID: 5–10 x 4–6m. Leaves palmate, deeply lobed, to 15 x 18cm, dark green. Flowers Jun–Oct, 7–10cm diam., bright yellow. Capsules to 9 x 6cm, brown, woody.

RANGE/HABITAT: Qld (Torres Strait Is to Bowen); also NG. Coast to ranges in woodland, rocky slopes and rainforest margins.

BEACH ALMOND *Terminalia catappa*

Excellent coastal shade tree with layered spreading branches and large leaves which turn bright red before falling. Almond-like yellowish fruit has edible kernel.

SIZE/ID:
12–20 x 10–20m. Deciduous. Leaves to 30 x 17cm. Flowers Oct–May, 1cm diam., cream/yellow, fragrant. Drupes to 8 x 5cm.

RANGE/HABITAT: Tropical Qld and NT; also Pacific Is, Asia. Beach scrubs, headlands and littoral rainforest.

NEW SOUTH WALES CHRISTMAS BUSH
Ceratopetalum gummiferum

The sepals of the small white flowers of this popular tree enlarge and turn bright pink/red as the fruit develop.

SIZE/ID: 4–10 x 2–5m. Leaves trifoliolate; leaflets to 8 x 5cm, margins toothed. Flowers Oct–Nov, 5mm diam., white. Sepals enlarge to 12mm long in Dec–Feb.

RANGE/HABITAT: NSW (Evans Head to Ulladulla). Coast to ranges in gullies in wetter forests.

DAVIDSON'S PLUM   *Davidsonia pruriens*

Unusual small tree cultivated for its sour acidic fruit that is made into jams, sauces and drinks.

SIZE/ID: 8–18 x 3–8m. Leaves pinnate, to 1.5m long. Leaflets to 45 x 16cm, drooping, hairy, margins toothed. Flowers 3–5mm diam., pink/red, pendulous spikes. Drupes to 5 x 6cm, purple/black, irritant hairs.

RANGE/HABITAT: Tropical Qld (Cooktown to Cardwell). Coast to ranges and tlnds in rainforest.

PENCIL PINE *Athrotaxis cupressoides*

Slow-growing, long-lived conifer (more than 1,000 years) that is highly fire-sensitive and only survives in some damp/wet, high-altitude regions in rocky or peaty soils.

SIZE/ID: 12–20 x 4–8m. Conical-shaped tree. Bark grey/brown, fibrous. Foliage green. Leaves scale-like, 2–3mm long, spirally arranged, single-veined. Male cones 3–5mm diam. Female cones 12–15mm diam., brown.

RANGE/HABITAT: Tas. Mountain rainforest and subalpine/alpine heath and scrub.

WHITE CYPRESS PINE *Callitris glaucophylla*

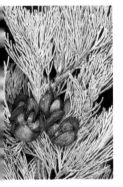

Common, slow-growing conifer that is widely distributed in inland regions, often in extensive stands. Timber valued for its termite resistance.

SIZE/ID: 12–20 x 8–12m. Dioecious. Bark dark, rough, furrowed. Foliage bluish grey. Leaves tiny, scale-like, triangular. Female cones 1.5–2.5cm across, grey/brown, woody, falling soon after maturity.

RANGE/HABITAT: Qld, NSW, Vic, SA, WA, NT. Inland hills and plains in sandy or rocky soil.

50 # TROPICAL CYPRESS PINE *Callitris intratropica*

Slow-growing conifer useful for shelterbelts and wood. Essential oils extracted from foliage. Aromatic timber is termite resistant.

SIZE/ID: 12–25 x 8–12m. Dioecious. Trunk single. Bark rough, grey, furrowed. Foliage dark green or bluish green. Leaves tiny, scale-like, triangular. Female cones 1–2cm diam., globose, woody, brown.

RANGE/HABITAT: Tropical Qld, NT, WA. Coast to ranges in heath, open forest and rainforest margins.

ROUGH TREEFERN *Alsophila australis*

Common, hardy treefern that often colonises moist sites on hillsides and disturbed areas, including roadsides and embankments. AKA *Cyathea australis*.

SIZE/ID: 8–20 x 6–9m. Trunk single, basal part with fibrous roots, upper part covered with rough/prickly petiole bases. Fronds bipinnate, emerging upright then spreading or drooping.

RANGE/HABITAT: Qld (se), NSW, Vic, Tas. Coast to ranges in wetter forests and fern gullies.

52 **COORANGOOLOO** *Elaeocarpus coorangooloo*

Impressive large tree with a dense shady canopy, masses of small but highly decorative flowers and colourful fruit. Leaves turn red before falling.

SIZE/ID: 20–30 x 10–20m. Leaves to 10 x 5cm, margins with blunt teeth. Flowers Jun–Sep, 6mm long, white or pink, petals fringed. Drupes to 1.5 x 1cm, blue.

RANGE/HABITAT:
Tropical Qld (Windsor Tlnd to Paluma). Ranges and tlnds in rainforest.

TROPICAL BLEEDING HEART *Homalanthus novo-guineensis*

Fast-growing tree which forms a spreading shady canopy. Frequently encountered in forest damaged by cyclones. Fruit and seeds eaten by birds.

SIZE/ID: 15–20 x 10–15m. Milky sap. Leaves to 20 x 20cm, heart shaped, senescing bright red. Flowers all year, 2mm diam., green/cream, scented. Fruit small, green to purple, with aril-bearing seeds.

RANGE/HABITAT: Tropical Qld, NT, WA; also NG. Wetter forests, including rainforest.

54 RED KAMALA *Mallotus philippensis*

Slow-growing bushy tree which has many medicinal uses.
Red dye from fruit. Seeds eaten by birds.

SIZE/ID: 15–25 x 10–15m. Leaves to 20 x 10cm, underside scaly/
hairy with red glands. Flowers all year, 3–5mm diam., cream/
yellow/brown, in spikes. Capsules 8–12mm diam., with red
glands, splitting to reveal blackish seeds.

RANGE/HABITAT: NT(n),
Qld, NSW (Torres
Strait Is. to Hunter R.);
also NG, Asia. Wetter
forests.

BLACK BEAN *Castanospermum australe*

Decorative bushy tree planted for the dense shade it provides.
Lorikeets feed on the flowers, often becoming intoxicated.

SIZE/ID: 15–30 x 10–20m. Leaves pinnate, to 40cm long. Flowers
Jul–Jan, 3–4cm long, red and orange/yellow, clusters on trunk
and large branches. Pods to 25 x 6cm, boat shaped, brown.

RANGE/HABITAT: Qld, NSW (Iron Range to Coffs Harbour);
also Pacific Is.
Coast to ranges in
rainforest.

56 BAT'S WING CORAL TREE *Erythrina vespertilio*

Hardy slow-growing tree with colourful, nectar-rich flowers. Usually leafless when flowering.

SIZE/ID: 5–12 x 5–10m. Bark cream/grey, corky. Trunk and branches thorny. Leaves bi- or trifoliolate (two subspecies), 10–15cm long. Leaflets to 10 x 12cm, shaped like bat's wing. Flowers Aug–Sep, 3–4cm long, red/scarlet, 10 protruding stamens. Pods to 15 x 2cm, red bean-like seeds.

RANGE/HABITAT: Qld, SA, WA, NT. Rocky outcrops, ridges and watercourses.

HOOKER'S BAUHINIA *Lysiphyllum hookeri*

Decorative tree with bushy crown, unusual leaves and attractive orchid-like white flowers. AKA *Bauhinia hookeri*.

SIZE/ID: 15–20 x 10–15m. Bark flaky. Leaves with kidney-shaped leaflets. Flowers 4–5cm diam., sweetly scented, white with pink/red stamens. Pods to 20 x 3.5cm, flat.

RANGE/HABITAT:
Qld (n to s), NT (n). Coast to ranges and west of dividing range in open forest, littoral rainforest and monsoon thickets.

58 **PONGAMIA** *Millettia pinnata*

Large deciduous tree with a dense, widely spreading shady
canopy. Popular in tropical coastal areas but can naturalise.
AKA *Pongamia pinnata*.

SIZE/ID: 10–20 x 15–25m. Young growth purplish. Leaves pinnate,
to 10cm long. Flowers Apr–Nov, 10–15mm long, pink/purple,
centre green, fragrant, in panicles. Pods to 9 x 3cm, indehiscent,
brown, woody.

RANGE/HABITAT: Qld (Torres Strait Is. to Paluma); also NG,
Pacific Is, Asia. Coastal rainforest.

NORTHERN LAUREL *Cryptocarya hypospodia*

Tall bushy tree suitable for planting in parks and large gardens. Fruit eaten by birds.

SIZE/ID: 15–25 x 10–18m. Leaves to 24 x 12cm, bright green, glaucous beneath. Flowers Nov–May, 4–5mm diam., green to cream/white, smelly, in panicles. Berries 15–18mm across, black, globose, can be ribbed.

RANGE/HABITAT: Qld (Cape York to Gympie), NT (rare); also NG. Coast to ranges in rainforest.

60 **ASIAN BARRINGTONIA** *Barringtonia asiatica*

Bushy shade tree with a spreading canopy, colourful new growth and fragrant flowers. The large, buoyant, lantern-like fruit, commonly seen on tropical beaches, have been used to stupefy fish.

SIZE/ID: 15–25 x 10–20m. Leaves to 40 x 17cm, bright green, shiny. Flowers in evening, Nov–May, 15–20cm diam., white with long pink stamens. Fruit to 10 x 10cm, brown/black.

RANGE/HABITAT: Qld (Cape York to Cairns), NT (n); also NG, India, Pacific Is., Madagascar. Beach scrub and mangroves.

MOODJAR *Nuytsia floribunda*

Bushy shrub/tree that is hemiparasitic on roots of adjacent plants. Spreads by suckers arising from very long, thick rhizomes. Flowers attract numerous insects and insectivorous birds.

SIZE/ID: 4–10 x 3–5m. Leaves to 100 x 8mm, dark green. Flowers Oct–Jan, 10–12mm across, brilliant yellow/gold/orange, in racemes to 25cm long.

RANGE/HABITAT: WA (Geraldton to Esperance). Coast to wheatbelt in sandplains and near rocks.

AUSTRALIAN BAOBAB *Adansonia gregorii*

Long-lived, slow-growing deciduous tree that develops a grotesquely swollen trunk (to 5m diam.) and thick spreading branches. Edible white tangy pith surrounds the seeds.

SIZE/ID: 5–15 x 8–15m. Leaves palmate. Flowers Dec–May,

6–7.5cm long, white, fragrant, opening at night. Pods to 18cm long, brown, woody, hairy.

RANGE/HABITAT: Tropical NT, WA. Coast to ranges in open forest, rocky hills and monsoon forest.

BROWN BOOYONG   *Argyrodendron trifoliolatum*

Imposing tree with a dense bushy canopy, massed floral displays and interesting, winged fruit. Useful for revegetation and streamside planting.

SIZE/ID: 15–40 x 8–20m. Trunk buttressed. Bark grey/brown, fissured. Leaves trifoliolate; leaflets to 15 x 6cm, brown scaly beneath. Flowers Dec–Jan, 15mm diam., bell shaped, cream/yellow, brown/scaly exterior, large panicles. Samara 4–6cm long, brown.

RANGE/HABITAT: Qld, NSW (Cooktown to Hastings R.). Coast to ranges in rainforest.

ILLAWARRA FLAME TREE *Brachychiton acerifolius*

Popular tree valued for its spectacular displays of massed coral
red flowers in large bunches over the entire canopy when leafless.

SIZE/ID: 10–35 x 10–15m. Leaves to 250 x 15cm, shiny, lobed.
Flowers Sep–Mar, 15–20mm diam., bright red. Follicles to 12 x
4cm, brown/black; seeds in rows.

RANGE/HABITAT: Qld, NSW (Iron Range to Illawarra). Coast to
ranges in rainforest.

BROAD-LEAVED BOTTLE TREE
Brachychiton australis

Notable tree with a sturdy trunk, ornamental leaves and decorative flowers that are particularly showy after leaf fall. Hardy shade tree for drier inland tropical areas.

SIZE/ID: 8–15m x 4–6m. Leaves to 20 x 20cm, green, lobed. Flowers May–Oct, 15–25mm diam., white interior, cream/yellowish exterior. Follicles to 10 x 4cm.

RANGE/HABITAT: Qld (Melville Range to Quilpie). Monsoon thickets and rocky hills.

LACEBARK TREE *Brachychiton discolor*

Popular ornamental tree with rounded/domed canopy, interesting leaves and colourful bell-shaped flowers which appear along the branches after leaf fall.

SIZE/ID: 10–30m x 10–20m. Leaves to 18 x 20cm, grey/white and hairy beneath, usually lobed. Flowers Nov–Mar, 50–80mm diam., bright pink, darker centre, hairy. Follicles to 15 x 5cm.

RANGE/HABITAT: Qld, NSW (Mackay to Dungog). Rainforest and monsoon thickets.

KURRAJONG *Brachychiton populneus*

Popular evergreen tree planted for its dense, bushy canopy. Important fodder tree, the foliage fed to stock during drought.

SIZE/ID: 10–20m x 8–12m. Leaves 5–10cm, often lobed. Flowers Nov–Mar, 10–15mm diam., bell shaped, cream/white with red marks. Follicles to 7 x 3cm.

RANGE/HABITAT: Qld (n to Townsville), NSW, Vic (ne and e). Coast to inland plains in woodland, mallee and dry rainforest.

QUEENSLAND BOTTLE TREE
Brachychiton rupestris

Distinctive tree with swollen, bottle-shaped trunk (to 2.5m diam. in old trees) and rounded to spreading crown. Planted as a feature tree, also for shade and stock fodder.

SIZE/ID: 10–20m x 10–15m. Deciduous. Leaves to 12 x 2.5cm, bluish beneath. Flowers Sep–Dec, to 10 x 18mm, unisexual, green/yellowish, occas. striped. Follicles to 3 x 2cm.

RANGE/HABITAT: Qld (Eungella to Goondoowindi). Rainforest and drier semi-deciduous forest.

BEACH HIBISCUS *Hibiscus tiliaceus*

Important, spreading tree for stabilising tropical beaches and tidal estuaries. Fast-growing and bushy to ground level. Withstands full coastal exposure.

SIZE/ID: 8–12 x 10–15m. Leaves to 30 x 25cm, heart shaped, underside white. Flowers Aug–Apr, 8–10cm diam., yellow with red centre, ageing redder.

RANGE/HABITAT: NT (n), Qld, NSW (Torres Strait Is. to Port Macquarie). Coastal and estuarine scrub, littoral rainforest.

NORFOLK ISLAND HIBISCUS
Lagunaria patersonia

Decorative tree planted in coastal areas. Valued for dense pyramidal shape and colourful flowers.

SIZE/ID: 10–20 x 8–15m. Young growth and leaves densely scaly. Leaves to 9 x 5cm, leathery. Flowers Nov–Feb, 2–2.5cm diam., pink with yellow stamens. Capsules to 3cm long, brown, irritant hairs.

RANGE/HABITAT: Norfolk Is, Lord Howe Is (widely naturalised on mainland Australia). Coastal scrub and rainforest.

WHITE CEDAR   *Melia azederach*

Fast-growing deciduous tree with widely spreading shady canopy. Popular in drier inland towns. Profuse displays of strongly scented flowers coincide with new leaf growth.

SIZE/ID: 20–40 x 20–35m. Leaves bipinnate, to 80 x 50cm. Flowers Aug–Dec, 1.5–2cm diam., blue/purple/cream, large clusters. Drupes to 4 x 2cm, yellow to brown.

RANGE/HABITAT: Qld, NSW (Cooktown to Milton); also NG, Asia. Coast to ranges in rainforest.

72 RED CEDAR *Toona ciliata*

Fast-growing deciduous tree with spreading shady canopy and valuable red timber.

SIZE/ID: 20–50 x 15–30m. Leaves pinnate, to 90cm long. Leaflets to 15 x 5cm. Flowers Sep–Nov, 6–10mm diam., white/cream, fragrant, terminal clusters. Capsules to 2 x 1cm, brown, opening star-like to release winged seeds.

RANGE/HABITAT: Qld, NSW (Iron Range to Milton); also NG, Asia. Coast to ranges in wetter forests.

TWO-VEINED HICKORY *Acacia binervata*

Fast-growing bushy tree planted for its ornamental qualities.
Also windbreaks and shelterbelts on rural properties.

SIZE/ID: 5–15 x 4–10m. Phyllodes to 14 x 3cm, often curved, 2–3
veins prominent. Flowers Aug–Nov, cream/pale yellow, globose
heads 5–10mm diam., profuse. Pods to 14 x 1.5cm, straight, flat.

RANGE/HABITAT: Qld, NSW (Springbrook to Narooma). Coast to
ranges in wetter forests.

COAST MYALL *Acacia binervia*

Highly ornamental bushy tree with decorative glaucous foliage
and massed displays of bright yellow flowers.

SIZE/ID: 5–15 x 4–10m. Phyllodes to 150 x 22mm, hairy, often
curved. Flowers Aug–Oct, cylindrical rods 3–6cm long, yellow.
Pods to 85 x 5mm, brown, straight or curved.

RANGE/HABITAT:
Qld, NSW (Ipswich
to Nungatta), Vic
(rare). Coast to
ranges in open
forest, often near
streams.

CEDAR WATTLE *Acacia elata*

Fast-growing, long-lived tree planted for shade, shelter and ornamental features. Honeyeaters feed on secretions from leaf glands, cockatoos and pigeons on the seeds.

SIZE/ID: 15–25 x 5–10m. Bark fissured, brown/black. Leaves bipinnate, to 30 x 30cm. Flowers Dec–Feb, cream/pale yellow, panicles of globose heads 7–10mm diam. Pods to 17 x 1.5cm, flat, dark brown.

RANGE/HABITAT: NSW (Bellingen to Milton). Wetter forests.

76 **IRONWOOD** *Acacia estrophiolata*

Slow-growing, hardy tree with weeping branches from semi-arid inland areas. By contrast, young plants have stiffly upright branches and clustered phyllodes.

SIZE/ID: 10–15 x 5–10m. Phyllodes to 11 x 0.5cm, often weakly kinked. Flowers after rain, cream/pale yellow, globose heads 4–5mm diam. Pods to 10 x 1cm, flat.

RANGE/HABITAT: Qld, SA, NT, WA. Sparse woodland and tall shrubland on sandy flats.

BROAD-LEAVED HICKORY *Acacia falciformis*

Slender bushy tree that can spread by suckers. Useful for
stabilising soil and embankments.

SIZE/ID: 5–12 x 4–8m. Bark grey/black, fissured. Phyllodes to
200 x 40mm, often curved. Flowers Aug–Oct, cream/pale yellow
globose heads 8–10mm diam. Pods to 12 x 2.5cm, greyish to
bluish, leathery.

RANGE/HABITAT: Qld,
NSW, Vic (Atherton
Tlnd to Traralgon).
Coast to ranges and
western slopes in tall
moist forest.

VELVET WATTLE *Acacia fulva*

Uncommon wattle with a restricted distribution. Fast-growing small tree valued for its decorative foliage and flowers.

SIZE/ID: 5–15 x 4–8m. Most parts velvety hairy. Leaves bipinnate, 5–10cm long, silvery hairy beneath. Flowers Nov–Jun, racemes of pale yellow globose heads 6–9mm diam. Pods to 12 x 6mm, leathery, dark brown.

RANGE/HABITAT: NSW (Gloucester to Mt Yengo). Ridges, slopes and gullies in open forest.

BRIGALOW *Acacia harpophylla*

Striking wattle that spreads by root suckers and often dominates extensive areas of scrub and forest. Commonest in semi-arid regions but coastal in some parts.

SIZE/ID: 15–25 x 10–20m. Bark blackish. Phyllodes to 30 x 3cm, silky hairy. Flowers Jul–Oct, golden/yellow, globose heads 5–8mm diam. Pods to 20 x 1cm, striate.

RANGE/HABITAT: Qld, NSW (Townsville to Roto). Open forest on fertile clay soils.

80 YARRAN *Acacia homalophylla*

Decorative small tree from inland
regions with rounded to spreading
canopy. Often multi-stemmed when
young. Suckers to form thickets.
Planted for shade, shelter and fuel.

SIZE/ID: 5–12 x 3–6m. Phyllodes to 100
x 7mm. Flowers Aug–Nov, bright yellow,
globose heads 4–6mm diam. Pods to
70 x 5mm, straight, papery.

RANGE/HABITAT: Qld, NSW (Emerald to
Tocumwal), Vic (n). Semi-arid woodland
on solonised soils and clays.

NELIA *Acacia loderi*

Hardy inland wattle that forms thickets by suckering and may dominate the shrubland in some areas. Planted as an ornamental.

SIZE/ID: 5–12 x 3–6m. Bark furrowed, fibrous. Phyllodes to 100 x 2mm, rigid, tip curved/hooked. Flowers Sep–Nov, golden yellow, globose heads 4–5mm diam. Pods to 100 x 5mm, constricted between seeds.

RANGE/HABITAT: NSW, SA, Vic (nw). Semi-arid woodland and shrubland on solonised soils.

82 **WEEPING MYALL** *Acacia pendula*

Majestic tree with a characteristic smell. Often grows in extensive stands. Planted for shade, shelter and ornamental features.

SIZE/ID: 5–15 x 3–5m. Bark grey, fissured. Branches pendulous. Phyllodes to 15 x 10mm, drooping. Flowers Feb–Apr, yellow, globose heads 5–7mm diam. Pods to 80 x 20mm, flat, greyish green.

RANGE/HABITAT: Qld, NSW, Vic (Emerald to Little Desert). Inland plains; often floodplains in heavy clay soil.

COOBA *Acacia salicina*

Graceful tree, common along stream banks, often forming
suckering colonies. Important for streambank stabilisation.
Attractive wood used for furniture.

SIZE/ID: 10–20 x 4–8m. Branches drooping. Phyllodes to 150 x
7mm, drooping. Flowers Feb–Jun, cream/pale yellow, globose
heads 7–10mm diam. Pods to 120 x 10mm, greyish, woody,
constricted between seeds.

RANGE/HABITAT: Qld, NSW, Vic, SA, NT. Western slopes to
inland plains in forest and shrubland.

WEEPING FIG   *Ficus benjamina*

Valued for its widely spreading shady canopy and weeping habit. Commonly planted in tropical parks and large gardens. Also trained as a decorative lollypop in urban areas.

SIZE/ID: 15–22 x 30–45m. Sap milky. Leaves to 12 x 6cm, with long pointed tip. Figs 8–12mm diam., ovoid, pink, red, purple or black.

RANGE/HABITAT: Qld (Cape York to Mackay), NT (n). Rainforest.

SMALL-FRUITED FIG *Ficus microcarpa*

Another large, spreading fig commonly grown in the tropics to provide shelter and shade. Birds feed on the small fruit.

SIZE/ID: 15–20 x 30–40m. Sap milky. Leaves to 12 x 9cm, elliptic, tip blunt. Figs 8–12mm diam., flattish, pink, purple, red or black.

RANGE/HABITAT: Qld (Cape York to Rockhampton); also NG, Pacific Is. Coast to ranges in rainforest.

PORT JACKSON FIG *Ficus rubiginosa*

Equally tolerant of coastal exposure and drier inland conditions, this adaptable fig provides valuable shade in summer.

SIZE/ID: 20–25 x 30–45m. Sap milky. Leaves to 20 x 12cm, rusty hairy beneath. Figs 1–2cm diam., yellow, orange, pink or red, often spotted.

RANGE/HABITAT: Qld, NSW (Torres Strait Is to Bega). Open forest, monsoon forest and rainforest, often among rocks.

STRANGLER FIG *Ficus* sp.

The photograph shows a species of *Ficus* growing as an epiphyte with its thick white roots strangling a tall rainforest tree. These roots suck nutrients from the host tree, which eventually dies, and the *Ficus* continues growing on its own. Several species of *Ficus* grow as stranglers in the rainforests of eastern Australia, from Torres Strait Is to Illawarra region. Birds disperse the small seeds in their droppings.

PEPPERMINT *Agonis flexuosa*

Bushy tree with weeping branches, tight clusters of white flowers and leaves that smell like peppermint when crushed. Often planted as an ornamental in streets, parks and gardens.

SIZE/ID: 5–15 x 5–10m.
Bark fibrous, brown, sometimes spiralled. Leaves to 15 x 1cm. Flowers Jul–Dec, c.1cm diam. Capsules 3–4mm diam.

RANGE/HABITAT: WA (Perth to Albany). Coastal dunes, heath and granite outcrops.

SMOOTH-BARKED APPLE *Angophora costata*

Often seen with a wonderfully gnarled trunk and crooked branches, this species also captures attention with colourful displays of shedding scaly bark and clusters of dense white fluffy flowers.

SIZE/ID: 15–25 x 10–20m. New bark pink/orange. Leaves to 20 x 3.5cm. Flowers Oct–Feb, c. 2.5cm diam., white. Capsules to 2 x 2cm.

RANGE/HABITAT: Qld, NSW (White Mtns to Narooma). Ranges to tlnds in forest.

GREY MYRTLE *Backhousia myrtifolia*

Dense, bushy, floriferous tree with cinnamon-scented leaves. Often grows naturally in dense stands near streams. Planted for wind protection, screening and hedging.

SIZE/ID: 15–25 x 6–12m. Bark brown, flaky. Leaves to 7.5 x 3.5cm. Flowers Nov–Jan, 1.5–2cm diam., white, starry, in large clusters. Capsules 5–6mm long.

RANGE/HABITAT: Qld, NSW (Fraser Is. to Bega). Coast to ranges in rainforest.

WILLOW BOTTLEBRUSH *Callistemon salignus*

Fast-growing bushy tree with dense foliage, flushes of pink new growth and attractive cream/yellow scented flowers. Birds feed in the flowers. AKA *Melaleuca salicina*.

SIZE/ID: 5–15 x 4–8m. Bark papery, peeling. Branchlets drooping. Leaves to 90 x 12mm. Flowers Sep–Nov. Capsules 5mm diam.

RANGE/HABITAT: Qld, NSW (Bundaberg to Timbillica). Moist/wet flats and streambanks in heavy soil.

WEEPING BOTTLEBRUSH *Callistemon viminalis*

This widely distributed and variable species is cherished for its displays of brilliant red bottlebrush-like flowers which attract birds. AKA *Melaleuca viminalis*.

SIZE/ID: 5–10 x 3–5m. Bark hard, furrowed. Branchlets drooping. Leaves to 70 x 7mm. Flowers Sep–Jan. Capsules 5mm diam.

RANGE/HABITAT: WA (n), Qld, NSW (Cape York to Gloucester). Coast to ranges and tlnds in open forest and rainforest, often in moist/ wet sites.

DESERT GHOST GUM *Corymbia aparrerinja*

Stunning tree that is widely distributed in arid regions of central Australia, where it shows off spectacularly against the red soils and rocky outcrops.

SIZE/ID: 10–20 x 10–15m. Bark smooth, white, powdery, scaly. Leaves to 16 x 3cm. Flowers Jul–Feb, 1.5cm diam., white, axillary clusters. Capsules to 1 x 1cm.

RANGE/HABITAT: Qld, NT, WA. Rocky hills, sandplains and near ephemeral streams.

94 MARRI *Corymbia calophylla*

Variable in habit, but commonly seen in parks and gardens as a
small tree with a bushy spreading canopy. Red sap oozes from
wounds.

SIZE/ID: 15–40 x 10–20m. Bark rough, grey/brown. Leaves to
18 x 3cm. Flowers Feb–May, 3–4cm diam., white/cream, rarely
pink, large terminal clusters. Capsules (honky nuts) to 5 x 4cm,
constricted near apex.

RANGE/HABITAT: WA (Geraldton to Albany). Near-coastal forest.

LEMON-SCENTED BLOODWOOD
Corymbia citriodora

Imposing tree that is widely planted for its open habit, stark white trunk and branches, and contrasting, dark green, lemon-scented foliage.

SIZE/ID: 20–40 x 10–25m. Bark smooth, dimpled, curling in strips. Leaves to 22 x 3cm. Flowers Jun–Nov, 2–2.5cm diam. Capsules to 1.5 x 1.2cm, barrel shaped.

RANGE/HABITAT: Qld, NSW (Laura to Coffs Harbour). Coast to inland ranges in open forest.

DALLACHY'S GHOST GUM *Corymbia dallachiana*

Impressive tree with attractive pale blotchy trunk, dense crown of leaves and showy floral displays which attract insects, birds and flying-foxes.

SIZE/ID: 20–40 x 10–25m. Bark smooth, cream/white/pinkish with resin streaks. Leaves to 27 x 3.5cm, margins often wavy. Flowers Nov–Dec, 1.5–2cm diam., cream/white. Capsules to 13 x 10mm, cup shaped.

RANGE/HABITAT: Qld (Coen to Emerald). Ridges and plains in woodland.

YELLOW BLOODWOOD   *Corymbia eximia*

Bushy tree with impressive but short-lived displays of intensely white flowers densely crowded in conspicuous clusters on the outside of the canopy. Commonly planted in streets and parks.

SIZE/ID: 5–20 x 8–12m. Bark yellow/brown, rough, flaky. Leaves to 20 x 3cm, grey/green, leathery. Flowers Aug–Dec, 2.5–3cm diam. Capsules to 2.5 x 1.5cm, barrel shaped.

RANGE/HABITAT: NSW (Singleton to Nowra). Open forest on sandstone.

98 RED-FLOWERING GUM *Corymbia ficifolia*

Popular small tree that is widely planted in temperate regions for its dense habit and spectacular displays of colourful flowers.

SIZE/ID: 5–15 x 10–15m. Bark grey/brown, rough. Leaves to 15 x 5cm. Flowers Jan–Mar, 3–4cm diam., white, pink, orange or red, terminal clusters. Capsules to 4 x 3cm, urn shaped.

RANGE/HABITAT: WA (near Perth to Walpole and Stirling Ra.). Near-coastal forest.

PAPER-FRUITED BLOODWOOD
Corymbia kombolgiensis

Small slender tree that grows in specialised sandstone habitats.

SIZE/ID: 8–12 x 5–10m. Bark smooth, mostly white, sometimes with a basal skirt of rough brown bark. Leaves to 20 x 1cm, shiny. Flowers Aug–Nov, 1–2cm diam., white, terminal clusters. Capsules 1 x 1cm, cylindrical to barrel shaped.

RANGE/HABITAT: NT (n). Sandstone escarpments and plateaux.

100 ROUND-LEAVED BLOODWOOD *Corymbia latifolia*

Distinctive small tree widely distributed in the northern tropics.
Deciduous in the dry season. Flowers attract nectar-feeding birds.

SIZE/ID: 8–15 x 5–10m. Basal bark rough, scaly, orange/brown,
upper bark smooth, mostly white. Leaves to 16 x 12cm. Flowers
Jan–Dec, 1–1.5cm diam., white, crowded terminal clusters.
Capsules to 14 x 12mm, ovoid.

RANGE/HABITAT: Qld, NT, WA; also NG. Rocky slopes and flats in grassy woodland.

SPOTTED GUM *Corymbia maculata*

Stately tree with a bushy crown and pale, distinctly mottled/
patchy colourful bark that changes seasonally. Floral nectar
important for honeyeaters and Swift Parrots.

SIZE/ID: 30–50 x 20–35m. Bark smooth, dimpled. Leaves to 20 x
3cm. Flowers May–Sep, 1.5–2cm diam., white, terminal clusters.
Capsules to 1.5 x 1cm, barrel shaped.

RANGE/HABITAT:
NSW (Taree to
Bega), Vic (Orbost).
Coastal forests.

102 SWAMP BLOODWOOD *Corymbia ptychocarpa*

Straggly or spreading bushy tree widely planted in the tropics for its spectacular, nectar-rich flowers which attract insects, birds and flying-foxes.

SIZE/ID: 10–20 x 5–10m. Bark grey/brown, rough. Leaves to 45 x 12cm, leathery. Buds ribbed. Flowers Jan–Sep, 3–4cm diam., white/cream, pink or red. Capsules to 4.5 x 2.5cm, ribbed.

RANGE/HABITAT: Tropical Qld, NT, WA. Streams, springs and swamps in woodland.

ROUGH-LEAVED BLOODWOOD *Corymbia setosa*

Small tree with opposite pairs of rough, heart-shaped, grey/green, bristly leaves which impart a distinctive appearance to the canopy.

SIZE/ID: 3–8 x 2–5m. Bark brown, rough. Leaves retaining juvenile shape, to 8 x 3cm, base stem-clasping. Flowers Jun–Nov, 3–4cm diam., white, pink or red. Capsules to 3 x 2.5cm, urn shaped.

RANGE/HABITAT: Qld, NT (Tennant Ck to Musgrave). Sandplain, rocky hills and woodland.

104 INLAND BLOODWOOD *Corymbia terminalis*

Widely distributed in inland regions, this tree provides important shelter and food for insects, birds and possums.

SIZE/ID: 10–20 x 10–25m. Bark brown, rough, tessellated, upper branch bark often smooth. Leaves to 20 x 3cm. Flowers Mar–Oct, 2–3cm diam., white/yellowish/pinkish, dense terminal clusters. Capsules to 3 x 2cm, urn shaped.

RANGE/HABITAT: Qld, NSW, NT, SA, WA. Flats, rocky hills and sandplains in sparse woodland.

CARBEEN *Corymbia tessellaris*

Decorative tree commonly planted in parks and windbreaks.
Heavy wood used for construction.

SIZE/ID: 20–35 x 20–30m. Trunk with basal skirt of tessellated
blackish bark, upper bark smooth, grey/white. Leaves to 24 x
2.5cm. Flowers Jan–Dec, 1.5cm diam., white, axillary clusters.
Capsules to 12 x 7mm.

RANGE/HABITAT: Qld, NSW (Torres Strait Is to Narrabri); also NG.
Plains and streambanks in open forest and coastal rainforest.

106 BLAKELY'S RED GUM *Eucalyptus blakelyi*

Majestic tree often retained in paddocks and planted in
shelterbelts, windbreaks and parks. Valuable hard timber and
nectar for honey production.

SIZE/ID: 15–25 x 20–20m. Bark smooth, white/grey/yellow.
Leaves to 16 x 2cm. Flowers Aug–Dec, 1–1.5cm diam., white
or pink, axillary clusters. Capsules 6–8mm diam.

RANGE/HABITAT: Qld, NSW, ACT, Vic. Woodland and swamps on
ranges and tlnds.

RIVER RED GUM *Eucalyptus camaldulensis*

Charismatic tree often associated with images and paintings of inland streams. The most widely distributed eucalypt. Valuable hard timber. Withstands flooding.

SIZE/ID: 15–35 x 20–35m. Bark smooth, white/grey/blue/pink. Leaves to 25 x 2cm. Flowers Jan–Dec, 1.5cm diam., white, axillary clusters. Capsules 5–9mm diam.

RANGE/HABITAT: Qld, NSW, ACT, Vic, SA, WA, NT. Streambanks, riverine forest and seasonally wet woodland.

108 ARGYLE APPLE *Eucalyptus cinerea*

Ornamental tree with attractive silvery/blue foliage that is
often bushy to ground level. Planted in streets, parks and larger
gardens.

SIZE/ID: 10–15 x 10–15m. Bark thick, rough, grey/brown, furrowed.
Leaves to 11 x 3cm, rounded juvenile leaves often mixed with
adult leaves. Flowers May–Nov, 1cm diam., white, small axillary
clusters. Capsules 9mm diam.

RANGE/HABITAT: NSW, Vic (Sofala to Beechworth). Open forest.

NEW ENGLAND MALLEE ASH
Eucalyptus codonocarpa

Decorative small tree with slender trunks, smooth bark and glossy green leaves. AKA *Eucalyptus approximans* subsp. *codonocarpa*.

SIZE/ID: 3–6 x 4–6m. Multi-trunked mallee with lignotuber. Bark grey/white/pinkish. Leaves to 15 x 2cm. Flowers Mar–Jun, 1cm diam., white, small axillary clusters. Capsules 8mm diam., barrel shaped.

RANGE/HABITAT: Qld, NSW (Mt Norman to Ebor). Shrubland on rocky ridges, mountain tops and granite outcrops.

110

BALD ISLAND MARLOCK
Eucalyptus conferruminata

Popular small ornamental tree valued for its spreading bushy habit and impressive heads of nectar-rich flowers.

SIZE/ID: 5–10 x 10–15m. Bark smooth, yellow/brown/grey. Leaves to 7 x 2cm. Flowers Aug–Mar, greenish yellow, fused into heads 8–10cm across. Capsules fused into head 4–6cm across.

RANGE/HABITAT: WA (Albany to Esperance). Flats and gullies in coastal forest and granite outcrops.

COOLABAH *Eucalyptus coolabah*

Slow-growing, long-lived tree of iconic significance in semi-arid inland areas because of its association with the Burke and Wills expedition.

SIZE/ID: 10–15 x 10–15m. Basal bark thick, grey, upper bark smooth. Leaves to 17 x 3cm. Flowers Jan–Dec, 1cm diam., white, terminal clusters. Capsules to 5 x 5mm, hemispherical.

RANGE/HABITAT: Qld, NSW, Vic, SA, WA, NT. Grassy woodland near streams, often heavy clay soil.

112 **ROUND-LEAVED GUM** *Eucalyptus deanei*

Tall and straight in dense forest, this species is shorter with a spreading crown in open habitats. Notable large old trees in the Blue Mtns.

SIZE/ID: 20–40 x 10–20m. Bark smooth, cream/pink/red. Juvenile leaves rounded. Mature leaves to 18 x 4cm. Flowers Feb–May, 1cm diam., white, axillary clusters. Capsules 5–6mm diam., bell shaped.

RANGE/HABITAT: Qld, NSW (Inglewood to Picton). Valleys and ridges in moist forest.

REDHEART *Eucalyptus decipiens*

Small tree with a spreading canopy. Planted in shelterbelts, windbreaks and regeneration projects.

SIZE/ID: 5–12 x 5–10m. Mallee or single-trunked tree. Bark grey, thick, rough. Juvenile leaves heart shaped. Adult leaves to 12 x 3cm. Flowers Aug–Jan, 1cm diam., white, dense axillary clusters. Capsules 5–6mm long, dense clusters.

RANGE/HABITAT: WA (Jurien Bay to Katanning). Sandplains, swamp margins and seasonally wet sites.

114 **KARRI** *Eucalyptus diversicolor*

Gigantic tree from high-rainfall regions. Often grows in pure stands. Important timber tree and an imposing feature for parks and acreage gardens.

SIZE/ID: 30–70 x 20–35m. Bark smooth, grey/cream to yellow/orange. Leaves to 12 x 3.5cm. Flowers Apr–Feb, 1–2cm diam., white, axillary clusters. Capsules to 1.2 x 1cm.

RANGE/HABITAT:
WA (Nannup to Mt Manypeaks). Near-coastal high-rainfall forests.

BROAD-LEAVED RED IRONBARK
Eucalyptus fibrosa

Hardy tree often seen on roadsides and retained in paddocks. Useful for honey and very hard, dark red wood.

SIZE/ID: 15–30 x 10–25m. Bark rough, deeply ridged, grey/black. Juvenile leaves to 14cm wide. Adult leaves to 20 x 5cm. Flowers Jan–Dec, 1.5–2cm diam., white. Capsules to 12 x 10mm, pear shaped.

RANGE/HABITAT: Qld, NSW (Rockhampton to Moruya). Coast to ranges and tlnds in open forest.

TASMANIAN BLUE GUM *Eucalyptus globulus*

Handsome, fast-growing tree often seen in parks, large gardens and rural properties. Important for forestry and hardwood plantations.

SIZE/ID: 25–45 x 10–25m. Basal bark mostly smooth, cream/grey/yellowish. Seedlings have square stems and large bluish leaves. Adult leaves to 30 x 5cm. Buds and capsules bluish, warty. Flowers May–Jan, 3–4cm diam., white/cream. Capsules to 2.5cm diam.

RANGE/HABITAT: NSW, Vic, Tas. Wetter forests.

TUART *Eucalyptus gomphocephala*

Grows as an impressive tall tree with a straight trunk in wetter forest but can also be straggly or multi-stemmed in harsh exposed sites.

SIZE/ID: 25–40 x 10–25m. Bark rough, thick, grey. Leaves to 18 x 5cm. Buds mushroom shaped. Flowers Jan–Apr, 2.5–3cm diam., white, strongly scented. Capsules to 18 x 18mm, bell shaped.

RANGE/HABITAT: WA (Jurien Bay to Ludlow). Coastal forests on sand.

ROSE GUM, FLOODED GUM *Eucalyptus grandis*

Towering tree widely planted in tropical countries for its timber, but also popular for shelterbelts and windbreaks on rural properties.

SIZE/ID: 35–60 x 25–40m. Bark smooth, white/grey/green. Leaves to 15 x 3cm. Buds and capsules bluish. Flowers Apr–Aug, 2–2.5cm diam., white, axillary clusters. Capsules to 8 x 5mm.

RANGE/HABITAT: Qld, NSW (Mt Windsor Tlnd to Newcastle). Wetter forests.

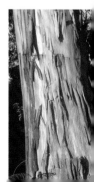

TABLELAND RED GUM *Eucalyptus interstans*

Crooked tree that often grows on rocky slopes and ridges
in shallow sandy soil. Patterns of colour in the bark change
seasonally.

SIZE/ID: 10–25 x 10–15m. Bark smooth, mottled/blotchy, white/
grey/brown/yellowish. Leaves to 20 x 3.5cm. Flowers May–Jul,
1.5cm diam., white,
axillary clusters.
Capsules to 8 x 9mm,
cup shaped.

RANGE/HABITAT:
Qld, NSW (Warwick
to Emmaville).
Woodland and open
areas on tlnds.

INLAND RED BOX *Eucalyptus intertexta*

Usually a sturdy tree but sometimes straggly and occasionally a mallee. Widely distributed in arid and semi-arid inland regions.

SIZE/ID: 10–25 x 10–20m. Basal bark rough, flaky, grey/red/ brown, upper bark smooth, pale. Leaves to 16 x 2.5cm. Flowers Feb–Dec, 1–1.5cm diam., white, terminal clusters. Capsules to 8 x 6mm, cup shaped.

RANGE/HABITAT: Qld, NSW, SA, WA, NT. Sparse woodland on open plains.

BLACK BOX *Eucalyptus largiflorens*

Significant tree of inland regions. Forms extensive stands on heavy soil in low-lying areas and withstands prolonged flooding. Excellent firewood. Flowers important for birds and honey production.

SIZE/ID: 10–20 x 10–20m. Bark rough, thick, hard, grey/black. Branches often drooping. Leaves to 18 x 2.5cm. Flowers Jan–Dec, 1cm diam., white. Capsules 4–5mm diam., cup shaped.

RANGE/HABITAT: Qld, NSW, Vic, SA. Woodland and floodplains.

YELLOW GUM *Eucalyptus leucoxylon*

Attractive bushy tree commonly grown in parks, gardens and rural properties for its colourful bird-attracting flowers. Important also for honey and durable timber.

SIZE/ID: 15–30 x 10–20m. Basal bark rough, upper bark smooth, cream/brown/bluish. Leaves to 20 x 3.5cm. Flowers Jan–Dec, 2.5–3cm diam., white, pink, red or yellow. Capsules to 12 x 12mm, barrel shaped.

RANGE/HABITAT: NSW, Vic, SA. Open forest and woodland.

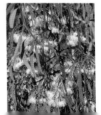

RED STRINGYBARK *Eucalyptus macrorhyncha*

One member of a group of trees which have persistent stringy bark over the trunk and branches. Often retained in paddocks and planted for shade and stock shelter.

SIZE/ID: 15–30 x 10–20m. Bark rough, grey/red-brown. Leaves to 15 x 3cm. Flowers Jan–Apr, 1–1.5cm diam., white/cream, axillary clusters. Capsules 1cm diam., globose, flattish.

RANGE/HABITAT: Qld, NSW, ACT, Vic, SA. Drier forest and woodland.

124 **SILVER-LEAVED IRONBARK**
Eucalyptus melanophloia

Decorative tree with silver/blue foliage that often grows in
prominent stands. Canopy consists mainly of juvenile leaves.

SIZE/ID: 15–25 x 10–15m. Bark rough, hard, deeply ridged, red/black. Juvenile leaves roundish, to 10cm wide. Adult leaves to 9 x 5cm. Flowers Jan–Dec, c.1.5cm diam., white. Capsules to 8 x 8mm, cup shaped.

RANGE/HABITAT: Qld, NSW (Mareeba to Dubbo). Drier forest and woodland inland from coast.

YELLOW BOX *Eucalyptus melliodora*

Important honey tree often retained during clearing operations
and surviving as relict trees in paddocks and along roadsides.

SIZE/ID: 15–30 x 20–30m. Trunk bark rough, grey/yellow/brown,
branches smooth, pale. Leaves to 14 x 2cm. Flowers Jan–Dec,
1.5cm diam., white/cream, rarely pink. Capsules to 7mm long.

RANGE/HABITAT: Qld, NSW, ACT, Vic. Woodland on slopes and
floodplains inland from
coast.

126 GREY BOX *Eucalyptus microcarpa*

Majestic tree often planted on rural properties for shade,
windbreaks and honey production. Important for wildlife. Useful
durable timber.

SIZE/ID: 10–25 x 10–20m. Bark rough, grey/white, small branches
smooth. Leaves to 15 x 3cm. Flowers Feb–Jun, 1.5cm diam.,
white, axillary clusters. Capsules to 9 x 5mm, cup shaped.

RANGE/HABITAT: Qld, NSW, Vic, SA. Grassy woodland on drier
western slopes and
inland plains.

TALLOWOOD *Eucalyptus microcorys*

Stately tall tree with reddish spongy/prickly bark, shiny, dark
green leaves and terminal clusters of white flowers. Often grows
in pure stands. Durable timber used in construction.

SIZE/ID: 30–60 x 20–40m. Bark rough. Leaves to 15 x 3.5cm.
Flowers Jan–Nov, 1.5cm diam. Capsules to 10 x 6mm.

RANGE/HABITAT: Qld, NSW (Toowoomba
to Cooranbong). Wetter forests on
valleys and mountains.

128 NEW ENGLAND PEPPERMINT *Eucalyptus nova-anglica*

Cold-tolerant tree with a bushy canopy of drooping bluish leaves. Planted for shade and shelter on rural properties and for regeneration.

SIZE/ID: 10–20 x 10–20m. Bark rough, grey/brown, deeply furrowed, branches smooth. Leaves to 19 x 1.5cm. Flowers Jan–May, 1cm diam., white, axillary clusters. Capsules 4–6mm diam., globose.

RANGE/HABITAT: Qld, NSW (Stanthorpe to Nowendoc). Woodland and open forest, often swampy.

SWAMP YATE *Eucalyptus occidentalis*

Useful tree for shelter, shade, fuel and honey. Tolerates wet soils, alkaline soils and salinity.

SIZE/ID: 10–20 x 5–12m. Basal bark rough, thick, grey/black, upper bark smooth, grey/white. Leaves to 12 x 3cm. Flowers Apr–Nov, 3–4cm diam., pale yellow, showy, axillary clusters. Capsules to 15 x 13mm, bell shaped.

RANGE/HABITAT: WA (Augusta to Israelite Bay). Near-coastal winter wet flats and lake margins.

130 **SNOW GUM** *Eucalyptus pauciflora*

Although commonest at high altitudes in cold montane habitats, this widely distributed decorative tree also occurs in near-coastal localities.

SIZE/ID: 10–20 x 8–15m. Bark smooth, white, grey or pale brown. Leaves to 20 x 5cm. Flowers Jan–Dec, 1.5cm across, white, axillary. Capsules to 1 x 1cm, cup shaped.

RANGE/HABITAT: Qld, NSW, Vic, Tas, SA. Coast to mountains and tlnds in forest.

BLACKBUTT *Eucalyptus pilularis*

Fast-growing tall tree grown in forestry plantations and on rural properties. Timber used for construction. Koalas eat the leaves.

SIZE/ID: 30–60 x 25–35m. Basal bark rough, fibrous, grey/brown, upper bark smooth, pale, scribbly. Leaves to 19 x 3cm. Flowers Jan–Dec, 1.5cm diam., white, axillary clusters. Capsules to 1 x 1cm, hemispherical.

RANGE/HABITAT: Qld, NSW (Fraser Is. to Eden). Coast to ranges in wetter forests.

WHITE GUM, POPLAR GUM
Eucalyptus platyphylla

Decorative tropical tree with smooth, white powdery bark and roundish green to grey/green leaves. Sometimes grows in pure stands. Deciduous in dry season.

SIZE/ID: 10–20 x 10–15m. Leaves to 20 x 12cm. Buds globose, clustered. Flowers Jun–Oct, 1.5cm diam., white, dense axillary clusters. Capsules to 6 x 10mm, hemispherical.

RANGE/HABITAT: Qld (Torres Strait Is. to Rockhampton). Open forest and grassy woodland.

RED BOX *Eucalyptus polyanthemos*

Slow-growing tree that withstands dryness and infertile stony soil. Often found in pure stands.

SIZE/ID: 10–25 x 10–15m. Basal bark rough, grey, upper bark smooth, mottled grey/cream/pink. Leaves to 11 x 5cm, blue/grey/green. Flowers Sep–Nov, 12mm diam., white/cream, terminal clusters. Capsules to 6 x 6mm, barrel shaped.

RANGE/HABITAT: NSW, Vic (Gulgong to Bendigo). Forest and woodland away from the coast.

134 **POPLAR BOX** *Eucalyptus populnea*

Hardy tree of inland areas, used for shade, shelter, wood and
honey. Koalas eat the leaves.

SIZE/ID: 10–20 x 10–15m. Basal bark rough, grey/brown, small
branches smooth. Juvenile leaves to 10cm across, roundish.
Adult leaves to 11 x 5cm, roundish. Flowers May–Dec, 1cm diam.,
white. Capsules to 3 x 3mm, hemispherical.

RANGE/HABITAT: Qld,
NSW (Rockhampton to
Narranderra). Grassy
woodland and open
forest.

SILVER-LEAVED MOUNTAIN GUM
Eucalyptus pulverulenta

Popular garden plant grown for its open growth habit and decorative silvery foliage.

SIZE/ID: 6–10 x 3–6m. Straggly tree, often multi-stemmed. Bark smooth, grey/ brown. Leaves to 5 x 5cm, mostly juvenile (adult leaves rare), rounded. Flowers May–Nov, 1.5cm diam., white, axillary clusters. Capsules 1cm long, bluish.

RANGE/HABITAT: NSW (Blue Mtns to near Bombala). Isolated populations on ridges in mountainous forest.

136 **INLAND SCRIBBLY GUM** *Eucalyptus rossii*

Highly decorative tree with distinctive white trunk that is usually marked by scribbly insect tracks in the bark.

SIZE/ID: 10–20 x 10–15m. Bark smooth, white/yellowish, powdery. Leaves to 17 x 1.3cm. Flowers Sep–Feb, c.15mm diam., white, axillary clusters. Capsules to 5 x 6mm, hemispherical.

RANGE/HABITAT: NSW (Tenterfield to Bombala), ACT. Forests on ridges and tlnds.

SYDNEY BLUE GUM   *Eucalyptus saligna*

Fast-growing tall tree with a spreading shady crown. Important
timber resource.

SIZE/ID: 25–45 x 20–30m. Basal bark rough, upper bark smooth,
white to blue/grey. Leaves to 20 x 4cm. Flowers Dec–Apr,
1.5–2cm diam., white, axillary clusters. Capsules to 8 x 8mm,
pear shaped, green.

RANGE/HABITAT: Qld, NSW
(Eungella to Sydney).
Wetter forests.

138 SALMON GUM *Eucalyptus salmonophloia*

Notable tree with appealing shape, decorative trunk and dense shady canopy. Valuable honey tree. Old bark, shed as flakes in summer/autumn, is replaced by new salmon-coloured bark.

SIZE/ID: 15–30 x 10–20m. Bark smooth, grey to grey/brown. Leaves to 12 x 1.5cm, very shiny. Flowers Jan–Oct, 1.5cm diam., white/cream, axillary. Capsules to 5 x 5mm, hemispherical.

RANGE/HABITAT: WA (Perth to Kalgoorlie). Woodland.

FLUTED GUM *Eucalyptus salubris*

Stunning tree with distinctive shiny bark which ranges from grey/
green to coppery brown. Valuable honey tree.

SIZE/ID: 10–20 x 8–15m. Young trunks slender, twisted/fluted.
Bark smooth, shiny, brown to coppery/brown. Leaves to 10 x
1.5cm, shiny. Flowers Sep–Mar, 2cm diam., white/cream, showy.
Capsules to 6 x 8mm, hemispherical.

RANGE/HABITAT: WA (Mullewa to Pingrup, inland to Laverton).
Woodland.

140 WALLANGARRA WHITE GUM *Eucalyptus scoparia*

Decorative gum with a restricted natural distribution. Popular cold-tolerant ornamental tree planted in gardens, parks and streets in temperate regions.

SIZE/ID: 10–20 x 8–15m. Bark smooth, white/grey, powdery.

Leaves to 15 x 1.5cm, pendulous. Flowers Nov–Dec, 1.5cm diam., white, axillary clusters. Capsules to 5 x 5mm, cup shaped.

RANGE/HABITAT: Qld, NSW (Wallangarra to Tenterfield). Granite peaks.

RED IRONBARK *Eucalyptus sideroxylon*

Popular for its colourful bird-attracting flowers, this stately ironbark is often planted around inland towns and rural properties.

SIZE/ID: 15–30 x 10–20m. Bark rough, hard, blackish. Leaves to 15 x 2cm. Flowers Apr–Dec, 1.5–2cm diam., white, pink or red, showy. Capsules to 1 x 1cm, barrel shaped.

RANGE/HABITAT: Qld, NSW, Vic. (Carnarvon Ra. to Horsham). Inland forests.

142 **JILLIGA ASH** *Eucalyptus stenostoma*

Distinctive tree with clusters of white flowers and capsules that contrast with the dark green leaves.

SIZE/ID: 10–25 x 5–15m. Basal bark rough, grey/black, upper bark smooth, pale, scribbly. Branchlets whitish. Leaves to 19 x 3cm. Flowers Sep–Dec, 15mm diam. Capsules to 1 x 1cm, globose.

RANGE/HABITAT: NSW (Tuross and Deua River catchments). Localised dense stands on forested ridges in shallow rocky soils.

FOREST RED GUM *Eucalyptus tereticornis*

Majestic tree widely planted in windbreaks and parks. Koalas eat the leaves. Durable wood used for construction.

SIZE/ID: 25–45 x 20–30m. Bark smooth, mottled, white to blue/grey/pink. Leaves to 20 x 3.5cm. Flowers Jan–Nov, 1.5cm diam., white, occasionally pink. Capsules to 6 x 8mm, ovoid.

RANGE/HABITAT: Qld, NSW (Cape York Peninsula to Bega); also NG. Forest and rainforest on slopes and plains.

144 **LAPUNYAH** *Eucalyptus thozetiana*

Attractive tree with white or weakly spotted trunk and dense bright green crown. Hard, durable, dark brown timber.

SIZE/ID: 15–25 x 10–15m. Trunk fluted at base. Bark smooth, white/pink, occasional rough basal stocking. Leaves to14 x 2cm. Flowers Mar–Nov, 1.5cm diam., white. Capsules to 5 x 5mm, urn shaped.

RANGE/HABITAT: Qld (Emerald to Quilpie), NT (near Arltunga). Low hills and rises in woodland.

GREEN MALLEE *Eucalyptus viridis*

Grown commercially for extraction of leaf oils, this small tree is
also an important honey tree and popular garden plant.

SIZE/ID: 5–12 x 5–8m. Trunk(s) slender. Basal bark rough, upper
bark smooth, pale. Leaves to 10 x 0.5cm. Flowers Feb–Dec,
1–1.5cm diam., white, axillary clusters. Capsules to 3 x 3mm,
globose.

RANGE/HABITAT: Qld
(n to Taroom), NSW, Vic,
SA (se). Woodland on
plains.

146 **WANDOO** *Eucalyptus wandoo*

Decorative tree that often grows in pure stands. Planted in parks, roadsides and rural properties. Durable pale brown wood used for construction. Valuable honey produced from its nectar.

SIZE/ID: 15–30 x 10–20m. Bark smooth, mottled, grey/white to yellow/brown. Leaves to 12 x 2.5cm. Flowers Jan–Oct, 3–4cm diam., white, showy. Capsules to 10 x 8mm, cylindrical.

RANGE/HABITAT: WA (Morawa to Pallinup). Woodland.

LEMON-FLOWERED GUM *Eucalyptus woodwardii*

Popular small tree planted in drier regions for its colourful flowers that attract nectar-feeding birds.

SIZE/ID: 5–15 x 5–10m. Bark smooth, grey, shedding in long ribbons to reveal white/pink new bark. Branches often pendulous. Leaves to 15 x 4cm. Flowers Jul–Nov, 4–5cm diam., yellow, showy. Capsules to 15 x 15mm, bell shaped, powdery.

RANGE/HABITAT: WA (near Kalgoolie). Semi-arid desert scrub.

148 **BRUSH BOX** *Lophostemon confertus*

Distinctive, fast-growing bushy tree often planted as an
ornamental in streets, parks and gardens.

SIZE/ID: 15–35 x 10–20m. Basal bark rough, brown, upper bark
smooth, pinkish. Leaves to 17 x 4.5cm, 3–5 at ends of branchlets.
Flowers Oct–Dec, 15–20mm diam., white, crowded clusters.
Capsules 8–12mm diam.

RANGE/HABITAT: Qld,
NSW (Cooktown to
Hunter R.). Coast
to ranges in wetter
forest.

SILVER PAPERBARK *Melaleuca argentea*

Decorative weeping tree with silvery foliage. Withstands wet soils and coastal conditions. Flowers attract birds and flying-foxes.

SIZE/ID: 15–25 x 10–15m. Bark papery, whitish. New shoots silvery/bluish, hairy. Leaves to 14 x 2cm. Flowers May–Nov, cream/yellowish, scented, crowded in bottlebrush-like spikes. Capsules 3–4mm diam., hairy.

RANGE/HABITAT:
Tropical Qld, NT, WA.
Streambanks and
riverine forest.

SALTWATER PAPERBARK *Melaleuca cuticularis*

Small tree, often multi-stemmed, with an open spreading canopy. Valuable for coastal stabilisation and revegetation projects. Tolerant of strong winds and saline soil.

SIZE/ID: 5–10 x 5–10m. Bark papery, white. Leaves to 12 x 3mm. Flowers Aug–Nov, white/cream, crowded in short spikes. Capsules 4–6mm diam., star shaped.

RANGE/HABITAT: WA (Perth to Israelite Bay), SA (Kangaroo Is.). Salt lakes, estuaries, seasonally wet areas, streambanks.

BLUE PAPERBARK *Melaleuca dealbata*

Handsome large tree that tolerates wet soils and coastal conditions. Flowers attract birds and flying-foxes.

SIZE/ID: 15–25 x 10–15m. Bark papery. Leaves to 12 x 3cm, bluish. Flowers Aug–Mar, white/cream, strongly scented, crowded in bottlebrush-like spikes. Capsules 4–5mm diam., hairy.

RANGE/HABITAT: Tropical Qld, NT, WA; also NG. Rainforest, swamps, seasonally wet sites in open forest.

152 **WEEPING PAPERBARK** *Melaleuca leucadendra*

Imposing tree popular in the tropics for its decorative papery bark, weeping habit and white/cream, sweetly scented, bottlebrush-like flowers.

SIZE/ID: 15–35 x 10–20m. Leaves to 20 x 2.5cm, light green. Flowers sporadically. Capsules 4–5mm across, glabrous.

RANGE/HABITAT: Tropical Qld, NT, WA; also NG. Rainforest, swamps, streambanks and seasonally wet sites in open forest.

STOUT PAPERBARK *Melaleuca preissiana*

Hardy tree with decorative bark and interesting growth features. Resprouts after fire and apparently tolerant of dieback disease induced by cinnamon fungus.

SIZE/ID: 5–10 x 5–10m. Bark papery. Branches often tortuous. Leaves to 15 x 2mm. Flowers Nov–Feb, cream/white, crowded in short spikes. Capsules 2–3mm diam.

RANGE/HABITAT: WA (Jurien Bay to Albany). Seasonally wet areas in coastal woodland and forest.

154 PRICKLY PAPERBARK *Melaleuca styphelioides*

Dense bushy tree that tolerates poor soils, salinity and urban
pollution. Valuable refuge plant for small birds.

SIZE/ID: 10–20 x 5–15m. Bark spongy, papery, white/brown.
Leaves to 15 x 5mm, prickly. Flowers Sep–Feb, white/cream,
crowded in bottlebrush-like spikes. Capsules 2–3mm diam.

RANGE/HABITAT: Qld, NSW (Rockhampton to Nowra). Moist/wet
areas in forest, swamps and along streamlines.

BROAD-LEAVED PAPERBARK
Melaleuca viridiflora

Straggly tree with an open canopy and massed displays of nectar-rich flowers.

SIZE/ID: 10–20 x 5–10m. Bark papery, cream/brown. Branches upright to weeping. Leaves to 20 x 6cm. Flowers sporadic, green, cream, yellowish, pink or red, crowded in showy bottlebrush-like spikes. Capsules 4–6mm diam.

RANGE/HABITAT: Tropical Qld, NT, WA; also NG. Wet areas in grassy woodland, swamps and rainforest.

156 TURPENTINE TREE *Syncarpia glomulifera*

Large tree with valuable timber that is resistant to termites and marine borers.

SIZE/ID: 20–40 x 15–25m. Bark grey/brown, furrowed, stringy. Leaves to 11 x 4.5cm, whitish-hairy underside, margins wavy. Flowers Oct–Dec, in fused clusters of 7, 1–2cm diam., white, scented. Capsules clustered.

RANGE/HABITAT: Qld, NSW (Cooktown to Bega). Coast to ranges and tlnds in wetter forests.

CREEK CHERRY *Syzygium australe*

Handsome bushy tree, widely grown and with several named cultivars available from nurseries.

SIZE/ID: 10–20m. Young growth bronze. Leaves to 10 x 35cm. Flowers sporadic, in clusters, each flower 10–12mm diam., white/cream. Berries to 20 x 15mm, pink/red, fleshy, edible.

RANGE/HABITAT: Qld, NSW (Cooktown to Nowra). Coast to ranges and tlnds in wetter forests, often along streams.

BUMPY SATINASH   *Syzygium cormiflorum*

Nectar-rich flowers of this interesting tree arise in clusters on the trunk and larger branches, followed by large unpalatable fruit.

SIZE/ID: 20–30 x 10–15m. New shoots pink/purple. Leaves to 21 x 11cm. Flowers Feb–Nov, 3–5cm diam., white/cream. Berries ovoid, to 6 x 3cm, white/cream or pink, fleshy.

RANGE/HABITAT: Qld (Iron Ra. to Townsville). Coast to ranges and tlnds in rainforest.

BUSH APPLE *Syzygium eucalyptoides*

Hardy tree from seasonally dry tropical regions that produces fruit eaten by many birds and animals.

SIZE/ID: 10–15 x 4–6m. Branches often pendulous. Leaves to 15 x 2cm, leathery. Flowers Aug–Oct, in clusters, each flower 10–15mm diam., cream/white. Berries to 40 x 40mm, white, pink or red, globose.

RANGE/HABITAT: Tropical parts of Qld, NT, WA. Streambanks and wettish sites in forest and woodland.

RIBERRY *Syzygium luehmannii*

Handsome tree valued for its dense habit, flowers and colourful fruit.

SIZE/ID: 10–15 x 8–12m. New growth pink/red or purplish. Leaves to 7 x 2.5cm. Flowers Oct–Dec, in crowded clusters, each flower 8–10mm diam., cream/white. Berries to 15 x 10mm, pear shaped, pink/red or purplish, fleshy, edible.

RANGE/HABITAT: Qld, NSW (Coen to Kempsey). Coast to mountains and tlnds in rainforest.

DUROBBY *Syzygium moorei*

Handsome tree with massed displays of colourful flowers along the larger branches, followed by clusters of fruit. Rare species due to loss of habitat.

SIZE/ID: 10–20 x 8–12m. Leaves to 16 x 8cm. Flowers Nov–Mar, crowded clusters along main branches, pink, showy. Berries to 30 x 50, flattish, globose, white/greenish, unpalatable.

RANGE/HABITAT: Qld, NSW (Gympie to Ballina). Coastal and near-coastal rainforest.

162 **MAGENTA CHERRY** *Syzygium paniculatum*

Uncommon bushy tree widely grown as an ornamental. Fruit eaten by possums and birds.

SIZE/ID: 5–15 x 5–10m. Leaves to 10 x 3cm, dark green, shiny. Flowers summer, in clusters, each flower 10–15mm across, white/cream. Berries to 20 x 20mm, globose, magenta, in dense clusters, edible.

RANGE/HABITAT: NSW (Taree to Conjola). Littoral rainforest and coastal scrub on dunes.

LILLY PILLY *Syzygium smithii*

Widely distributed species that exhibits variation in plant habit, leaf size and fruit colour.

SIZE/ID: 10–20 x 8–15m. New growth often pink/reddish. Leaves to 15 x 6cm. Flowers Nov–Feb, clusters, each flower 3–5mm across, white/cream. Berries to 1.5 x 1.5cm, flattish, white to purple, unpalatable.

RANGE/HABITAT: Qld, NSW, Vic (Windsor Tlnd to E Vic). Wetter forests, often along streams.

164 **WATER GUM, KANOOKA** *Tristaniopsis laurina*

Distinctive, long-lived, bushy tree with
blotchy pale bark, spreading branches and
shady canopy.

SIZE/ID: 15–25 x 10–15m. Trunk single or
multiple. Bark smooth. New growth often
pink/reddish. Leaves to 12 x 3cm. Flowers
Nov–Feb, 10–15mm diam., yellow, crowded
clusters. Capsules 4–6mm diam.

RANGE/HABITAT: Qld, NSW, Vic (Brisbane to
Gippsland). Coast to ranges in wetter forest
beside streams.

BEACH PANDAN *Pandanus tectorius*

Iconic coastal tree often seen in exposed sites by the sea. Separate male and female plants.

SIZE/ID: 5–12 x 4–8m. Trunk with long prop roots. Leaves spirally arranged, to 1.7m x 10cm, somewhat twisted, margins smooth or spiny. Flowers tiny, in terminal spikes. Fruit pineapple-like, to 18 x 13cm, ripening yellow/orange.

RANGE/HABITAT: Qld, NSW (Torres Strait Is. to Iluka). Coastal dunes and littoral rainforest.

166 **WHITE HOLLY** *Auranticarpa rhombifolia*

Narrow tree widely grown for its foliage, flowers and massed displays of colourful fruit.

SIZE/ID: 15–25 x 10–20m. Bark grey, corky. Leaves to 12 x 7cm, broadly toothed. Flowers Oct–Feb, 10–12mm diam., white, scented, showy clusters. Capsules to 10 x 8mm, orange, splitting to display black seeds.

RANGE/HABITAT: Qld, NSW (40-Mile Scrub to Alstonville). Coast to low ranges in rainforest and woodland.

NATIVE FRANGIPANI *Hymenosporum flavum*

Popular bushy tree with dark green foliage and contrasting displays of sweetly scented yellow and white flowers.

SIZE/ID: 8–15 x 7–12m. Leaves to 20 x 5cm. Flowers Dec–Mar, 5–8cm diam., cream ageing to yellow, sweetly scented. Capsules 3–4cm long, brown, numerous winged seeds.

RANGE/HABITAT: Qld, NSW (Cooktown to Blue Mtns); also NG. Coast to ranges and tlnds in wetter forests.

PLUM PINE *Podocarpus elatus*

Slow-growing tree with a dense habit and edible, bird-attracting
fleshy receptacles that support the hard fruit.

SIZE/ID: 10–30 x 8–18m. Dioecious. Leaves to 18 x 1cm, yellowish
when young. Male cones 2–3cm long. Drupes 1.5 x 1cm, bluish,
powdery, attached to purple/black receptacle 2–2.5cm long.

RANGE/HABITAT: Qld, NSW (McIlwraith Ra. to Illawarra). Coast to
ranges in rainforest.

WEEPING BROWN PINE *Podocarpus grayae*

Handsome tree with flushes of pale green, new leaves and interesting fruiting structures that are eaten by birds.

SIZE/ID: 10–25 x 8–18m. Dioecious. Leaves to 25 x 2cm, dark green, shiny. Male cones 2–6cm long. Fruit to 2 x 1.5cm, bluish, powdery, attached to fleshy red receptacle.

RANGE/HABITAT: Tropical Qld. Coast to ranges and tlnds in rainforest.

170 **QUEENSLAND WARATAH** *Alloxylon flammeum*

Spectacular bushy tree that produces magnificent floral displays attracting numerous nectar-feeding birds. Soft timber is attractively patterned.

SIZE/ID: 15–30 x 8–12m. Leaves to 30 x 6cm, rusty/hairy beneath. Flowers Aug–Jan, brilliant red clusters on end of branches. Follicles to 10cm long, brown, opening to release brown winged seeds.

RANGE/HABITAT: Tropical Qld (Atherton Tlnd area). Rainforest, often on basalt.

ATHERTON OAK *Athertonia diversifolia*

Excellent shade tree with decorative foliage, colourful fragrant flowers, interesting blue fruit and edible seeds.

SIZE/ID: 15–25 x 8–12m. Leaves to 35 x 12cm, simple or lobed, paler beneath. Flowers Feb–Jun, white/cream, sweetly scented, in pendulous racemes to 55cm long. Drupes to 4 x 4 cm, blue/purple.

RANGE/HABITAT: Qld (Cape Tribulation to Malanda). Coast to ranges and tlnds in rainforest.

CANDLESTICK BANKSIA *Banksia attenuata*

Hardy, long-lived tree with spectacular displays of flowers. Regenerates after fire from basal lignotubers and internal buds in the trunk.

SIZE/ID: 4–10 x 3–8m. Trunk single or multi-stemmed. Bark orange/grey. Leaves to 25 x 1.5cm, margins toothed. Flowers Oct–Feb, bright yellow spikes to 30 x 5cm.

RANGE/HABITAT: WA (Kalbarri to Cape Leeuwin to Fitzgerald River). Woodland, shrubland and sandplain.

COASTAL BANKSIA *Banksia integrifolia*

Important coastal tree that withstands salt-laden winds and provides refuge and food for wildlife in autumn/winter when little else is available.

SIZE/ID: 5–30 x 5–12m. Bark grey, rough. Leaves in whorls, to 25 x 4cm, white beneath, stiff, margins smooth (juveniles toothed). Flowers Mar–Jul, yellow, in spikes to 12 x 5cm.

RANGE/HABITAT: Qld, NSW, Vic (Proserpine to Geelong). Coastal scrub on beaches, dunes and headlands.

174 OLD MAN BANKSIA *Banksia serrata*

Gnarled tree commonly seen in coastal areas but also extending to the ranges. Honeyeaters and cockatoos feed on the flowers and seeds.

SIZE/ID: 5–15 x 4–8m. Bark grey/brown, lumpy/warty. Leaves to 20 x 4cm, paler beneath, stiff, margins toothed. Flowers Jan–Jun, cream/grey/yellowish, in spikes to 20 x 10cm.

RANGE/HABITAT: Qld (s), NSW, Vic, Tas (n). Open forest, woodland and heath, often on dunes.

IVORY CURL TREE *Buckinghamia celsissima*

Bushy tree valued for its stunning floral displays. Widely planted in the subtropics but also adaptable in cooler climates.

SIZE/ID: 15–25 x 8–12m. Leaves to 20 x 7cm, rusty to silvery/white beneath. Flowers Jan–May, cream/white, fragrant, in arching racemes to 20cm long. Follicles to 3 x 2cm, brown, long curled tip.

RANGE/HABITAT: Qld (Cooktown to Paluma). Coast to ranges and tlnds in rainforest.

BROWN SILKY OAK   *Darlingia darlingiana*

Decorative tree valued for its open habit, flushes of new growth, interesting leaves and profuse flowering.

SIZE/ID: 15–25 x 8–12m. Leaves to 50 x 15cm, unlobed or with spreading lobes. Flowers May–Nov, white/cream, strongly scented, in spikes or panicles. Follicles to 7 x 3cm, brown, shedding winged seeds.

RANGE/HABITAT: Qld (Cooktown to Paluma). Coast to ranges and tlnds in rainforest and regrowth.

WHITE OAK   *Grevillea baileyana*

Bushy tree with decorative foliage which shows to effect on windy days. Massed flowering adds to the appeal. AKA *Grevillea edelfeltii*.

SIZE/ID: 15–30 x 8–15m. Juvenile leaves lobed. Mature leaves to 30 x 8cm, rusty hairy beneath. Flowers Aug–Dec, cream/white, scented, crowded racemes to 15cm long. Follicles to 2cm long, brown, shedding winged seeds.

RANGE/HABITAT: Qld (Bolt Head to Tully); also NG. Coast to ranges in rainforest.

WHITE YIEL YIEL *Grevillea hilliana*

Bushy tree with attractive foliage and interesting flowers. Leaves can be unlobed or have up to 10 spreading lobes.

SIZE/ID: 15–25 x 8–12m. New shoots rusty hairy. Mature leaves to 20 x 6cm, whitish beneath. Flowers Jul–Feb, cream/white, in racemes to 20cm long. Follicles to 3 x 2cm, brown.

RANGE/HABITAT: Qld, NSW (Cooktown to Mullumbimby). Coast to ranges in rainforest.

SILVER OAK *Grevillea parallela*

Decorative small tree suitable for ornamental planting in the tropics. Birds feed in the nectar-rich flowers.

SIZE/ID: 8–15 x 4–8m. Leaves to 40 x 1cm, drooping, silvery grey, leathery. Flowers May–Dec, cream/white, in racemes to 12cm long, often in dense clusters, attractively scented. Follicles to 2.5 x 1.5cm, grey/brown.

RANGE/HABITAT: Tropical Qld, NT, WA. Woodland, open forest and savannah.

180 **SILKY OAK** *Grevillea robusta*

Fast-growing tree that produces stunning displays of colourful flowers that attract an array of nectar-feeding birds. Naturalises readily.

SIZE/ID: 15–30 x 10–15m. Leaves fern-like, to 30 x 12cm, silvery beneath. Flowers Oct–Jan, golden/orange, conspicuous in racemes or panicles to 12cm long. Follicles 2 x 2cm, brown.

RANGE/HABITAT: Qld, NSW (Biggenden to Coffs Harbour). Coast to ranges in wetter forests.

NEEDLEWOOD *Hakea divaricata*

Slow-growing small tree from semi-arid inland regions. Insects and birds feed in the nectar-rich flowers.

SIZE/ID: 2–8 x 3–5m. Bark deeply furrowed, corky. Leaves needle-like, prickly, forked into spreading segments. Flowers Jun–Nov, yellow/green, crowded in spikes to 15cm long. Follicles to 4cm long.

RANGE/HABITAT: Central areas of Qld, NT, WA, SA. Sparse woodland in red sand, rockholes, rocky hills.

182 BOOTLACE OAK *Hakea lorea*

Distinctive long-lived tree from drier inland regions. Nectar-rich flowers attract birds and insects.

SIZE/ID: 2–10 x 4–8m. Bark deeply fissured, corky. Leaves upright or long and drooping, to 700 x 2mm. Flowers Apr–Sep, white or yellow, crowded in spikes to 25cm long. Follicles to 5cm long.

RANGE/HABITAT: Inland and northern Qld, NT, WA, SA. Drier plains and ranges in woodland.

FIREWHEEL TREE *Stenocarpus sinuatus*

Handsome rainforest tree grown for its decorative foliage and spectacular displays of brilliant red wheel-like flowers.

SIZE/ID: 15–35 x 8–15m. Juvenile leaves lobed. Mature leaves entire or lobed, to 45 x 25cm. Flowers Jun–Feb, bright red. Follicles to 10 x 2cm, brown, shedding winged seeds.

RANGE/HABITAT: Qld, NSW (Daintree to Nambucca); also NG. Ranges and tlnds in rainforest.

184 LEICHHARDT TREE *Nauclea orientalis*

Ornamental tree with spreading branches, shady canopy, strongly scented flowers and edible (but bitter) fruit.

SIZE/ID: 15–20 x 10–15m. Deciduous. Leaves to 30 x 18cm. Flowers Sep–Mar, crowded in spherical flowerheads 2–4cm diam., each flower orange with a protruding white style/stigma. Drupes 4–5cm across, brown, surface wrinkled/pocked.

RANGE/HABITAT: Tropical Qld, NT, WA; also NG, Asia. Streambanks and swamps in rainforest and thickets.

BASTARD CROW'S ASH *Flindersia collina*

Distinctive floriferous tree with a dense
shady canopy, attractive blotched bark
and unusual fruit.

SIZE/ID: 15–30
x 10–18m. Bark
dappled/spotted.
Leaves simple or
compound. Leaflets to 7 x 3cm. Flowers
Jun–Oct, 5–8mm diam., white/yellowish,
profuse in panicles. Capsules 3–5cm long,
brown, externally prickly, separating into
5 boat-shaped segments.

RANGE/HABITAT: Qld, NSW (Lakefield to Toonumbar). Monsoon
forest, vine thickets and dry rainforest.

186 **LEOPARDWOOD, BAGALA** *Flindersia maculosa*

Inland tree renowned for its striking bark.
Young plants form a tangled mass of thin spiny
branches before a main shoot emerges.

SIZE/ID: 8–15 x 5–8m. Bark dappled/spotted
orange and grey. Leaves simple, to 7 x 1cm.
Flowers Sep–Dec, 6–8mm diam., white/cream.
Capsules 2–2.5cm long, brown, externally
bumpy, 5 boat-shaped segments.

RANGE/HABITAT: Qld, NSW (Hughenden to Hay).
Inland semi-arid sandy plains and rocky hills.

SILVER ASH *Flindersia schottiana*

Fast-growing tree with a spreading shady canopy. Planted for shelter and wildlife.

SIZE/ID: 15–35 x 8–30m. Leaves pinnate, to 30cm long. Leaflets to 25 x 8cm. Flowers Dec–Apr, white, 4–6mm diam., honey-scented, large showy clusters. Capsules 8–12cm long, brown, externally spiny, 5 boat-shaped segments.

RANGE/HABITAT: Qld, NSW (Iron Range to Port Macquarie); also NG. Coast to ranges and tlnds in rainforest.

188 **WILGA** *Geijera parviflora*

Slow-growing, spreading tree of drier areas, valued for shade, shelter and stock fodder. Sheep level off the lower foliage of favoured trees.

SIZE/ID: 5–12 x 5–12m. Leaves drooping, to 25 x 1.5cm, spicy smell when crushed. Flowers Jun–Nov, 1cm diam., white, starry, yellow central disc, smelly. Follicles 4–5mm long, green/brown, splitting to expose shiny black seed.

RANGE/HABITAT: Qld, NSW, Vic, SA. Inland woodland.

BROAD-LEAVED BALLART   *Exocarpos latifolius*

Unusual slow-growing tree which survives as a hemiparasite on the roots of other plants.

SIZE/ID: 5–10 x 3–8m. Bark rough. Leaves to 14 x 7cm. Flowers Jan–Jul, 2–3mm diam., yellowish. Drupes 5–10mm long, red, sitting atop an edible, yellow/red, fleshy receptacle.

RANGE/HABITAT: Tropical WA, NT, Qld, NSW (Torres Strait Is. to Evans Head); also Malesia. Open forests and wetter forests.

190 **BOONAREE** *Alectryon oleifolius*

Small tree that can spread by suckers to form extensive clonal colonies. Three subspecies named. Leaves can be toxic to stock.

SIZE/ID: 5–10 x 8–12m. Bark grey/brown. Leaves to 14 x 1cm, green or bluish, veins prominent. Flowers small, green/yellow, small groups. Capsules green. Seed shiny, black with red aril.

RANGE/HABITAT: Qld, NSW, Vic, SA, WA, NT. Coastal plains (WA) to inland plains in woodland.

WHITEWOOD *Atalaya hemiglauca*

Hardy, small, drought tolerant, suckering tree valued by pastoralists for shelter and stock fodder.

SIZE/ID: 5–10 x 8–12m. Leaves pinnate, to 20 x 16cm. Leaflets to 15 x 1.5cm. Flowers 1–1.5cm diam., cream/white, large clusters. Samaras to 4 x 1cm, yellow/green, consisting of 1–3 winged fruitlets.

RANGE/HABITAT: Qld, NSW, SA, WA, NT. Semi-arid inland plains, sand ridges and vine thickets.

NATIVE TAMARIND *Diploglottis australis*

Ornamental tree from the rainforest with large decorative leaves and terminal panicles of flowers and fruit.

SIZE/ID: 15–30 x 10–20m. New growth rusty, hairy. Leaves pinnate, to 1.2m long. Leaflets to 30 x 8cm. Flowers Oct–Jan, 3–4mm long, cream/brown. Capsules 10–15mm across, 1–3-lobed, brown, hairy. Seeds with orange/yellow edible aril.

RANGE/HABITAT: Qld, NSW (Bunya Mtns to Brogo). Coastal hills and mountains in wetter forests.

WHITE SIRIS *Ailanthus triphysa*

Excellent shade tree that tolerates dry periods and exposed coastal conditions.

SIZE/ID: 25–40 x 20–30m. Bark sandpapery. Leaves pinnate, to 45 x 20cm, crowded at end of branches. Leaflets to 12 x 2cm, underside bluish. Flowers Sep–Dec, 1cm across, cream/green, in axillary panicles to 20cm long. Samaras to 6 x 2cm, pinkish/ brown, papery.

RANGE/HABITAT: Qld, NSW (Olive River to Iluka), WA(n). Coast to ranges in rainforest.

GRASS TREE *Xanthorrhoea johnsonii*

Widely distributed common grasstree. Birds and insects feed on the nectar-rich flowers.

SIZE/ID: 1–6m tall. Trunk slender, grey. Leaves in a bright green rounded crown, old leaves forming a grey/brown basal skirt. Inflorescence to 3.5m tall. Flowers white, spirally arranged in a dense cylindrical spike of similar length to the basal woody stem.

RANGE/HABITAT: Qld, NSW (Heathlands to Singleton). Coast to ranges and tlnds in open forest.

GLOSSARY

Axillary: Borne in an axil.

Aril: Outgrowth on a seed; often fleshy or colourful to encourage feeding by birds or insects.

Berry: A fleshy many-seeded fruit.

Bipinnate: Leaves twice pinnately divided.

Bisexual: Both male and female sexes present.

Calcareous: An excess of lime in a soil.

Capsule: A dry fruit that breaks open to release seeds.

Cladode: A modified stem acting as a leaf.

Compound leaf: A leaf with two or more separate leaflets.

Conifer: A cone-bearing tree with needle-like leaves.

Crownshaft: A structure on the top of a palm trunk formed by tightly packed tubular leaf bases.

Dioecious: Bearing male and female flowers on separate plants.

Drupe: A fleshy indehiscent fruit.

Eucalypt: General term for species of *Angophora*, *Corymbia* and *Eucalyptus*.

Genus: A taxonomic group of closely related species.

Glabrous: Without hairs.

Glaucous: Bluish to bluish-grey.

Gymnosperm: Vascular plant that produces exposed seeds (usually in cones).

Hemiparasite: Shrub or tree obtaining nutrients from another species.

Indehiscent: Not splitting open at maturity.

Leaflet: Segment of a compound leaf.

Lignotuber: Woody underground growth on mallee eucalypts from which new shoots can arise.

Littoral: Growing on the shores of a lake, sea or ocean.

Mallee: A eucalypt with multiple stems arising from at or below ground level.

Monocotyledon: Angiosperm plant with a single seed leaf and parallel venation.

Monoecious: Bearing male and female flowers on the same plant.

Nodes: Joints or thickenings along branches and branchlets where leaves arise.

Palmate: Palm shaped, divided like a hand.

Panicle: A branched inflorescence.

Papillate: With small, irregular, pimple-like bumps.

Petiole: The stem or stalk of a leaf.

Phyllode: A modified petiole acting as a leaf.

Pinnate: Once divided with the divisions extending to the central stem.

Plumose: Said of a compound leaf with leaflets arising in different directions.

Pod: A dry fruit that splits when ripe to release seeds.

Raceme: Unbranched inflorescence with stalked flowers.

Rachis: The main axis of a compound leaf or inflorescence.

Receptacle: Specialised fleshy fruit-supporting organ.

Reticulate: A network of veins.

Rhizome: An underground stem.

Saline: Salty, an excess of salt in a soil.

Samara: An indehiscent winged seed.

Scribbly: A term applied to tunnels formed by caterpillars feeding in the smooth bark of a eucalypt.

Sessile: Without a stalk.

Simple: Undivided, as in leaves.

Solonised: Said of soils containing large amounts of calcium and magnesium.

Species: A group of closely related plants with a common set of features that sets them apart from another species.

Spike: Unbranched inflorescence with sessile flowers.

Sucker: A shoot arising from the roots below ground level.

Tepals: Term used when sepals and petals are of similar shape, size and colour.

Terminal: At the end.

Tessellated: As if laid with a mosaic of uniform tiles.

Trifoliolate: Compound leaf with three leaflets.

Unisexual: Of one sex only, either male or female.

Whorl: More than two organs arising from the one place.

FURTHER READING

Allen, R, and Baker, K. 2014. *Australia's Remarkable Trees.*

Benwell, A. 2020. *Plants of Subtropical Eastern Australia.*

Boland, D J, and Brooker, M I H (eds). *Forest Trees of Australia.* CSIRO Publishing.

Brooker, M I H, and Kleinig, D A. 1983. *Field Guide to Eucalypts of South-eastern Australia.* Inkata Press.

Brooker, M I H, and Kleinig, D A. 1990. *Field Guide to Eucalypts of South-western and Southern Australia.* Inkata Press.

Brooker, M I H, and Kleinig, D A. 1994. *Field Guide to Eucalypts of Northern Australia.* Inkata Press.

Cronin, L. 2007. *Cronin's Key Guide to Australian Trees.*

Holliday, I. 2002. *A Field Guide to Australian Trees*, Reed New Holland Publishers.

Krish, P. 2015. *Green Guide: Trees of Australia.* Reed New Holland Publishers.

Simmons, M H. 1981. *Acacias of Australia.* Thomas Nelson Australia.

Simmons, M H. 1981. *Acacias of Australia, volume 2.* Viking O'Neil.

Wrigley, J, and Fagg, M. 2012. *Eucalypts: A Celebration.* Allen and Unwin.